LOUISIANA LEGACY

History of the
Daigle and Schexnayder Families

Cypress Cove Publishing

PRAISE FOR "LOUISIANA LEGACY"

Louisiana Legacy is a must read for anyone with an interest in Louisiana, it's people or its culture. Daigle masterfully penned a book that has the intricacies of a research piece while also keeping the reader invested with intriguing story lines. If you want a real, boots on the ground type look at Louisiana's formative years and growth to its current state, *Louisiana Legacy* should top your list.

Rob Landry, Manager of Public Affairs and Communication, Louisiana Chemical Association

I thoroughly enjoyed reading *Louisiana Legacy*. I was surprised to learn about the migration of French Acadians prior to the Grand Derangement and how the German immigrants melded with their French counterparts in Louisiana. My overall feeling was one of gratitude for the precious gift that your book is / will be to your children, grandchildren and so-on.

Arthur Price, VP of Finance, Badger Oil Co.

Eddie Daigle's look back at the Daigle and Schexnayder family histories from the late 1500s to modern times is a touching, well-researched gift to all of us in Louisiana – and a good history lesson as well. There can be no better time than the 250th anniversary of Acadians' arrival in South Louisiana to pen his excellent study.

Warren Perrin, Acadian Heritage and Culture Foundation

This is the story of us. No, not the Schexnaydre or Schexnayder family, nor is it the story of the Daigle family. This is the story of every family that arrived in colonial Louisiana before it was sold by France. While the details are specific to the aforementioned families, Eddie's journey from the origins of his paternal and maternal lineage through to his childhood in Garyville - is the story of South Louisiana. The overall history makes an enjoyable read for the casual historian, but the details are a treasure for those who share the Schexnayder and Daigle lineage.

Jay Schexnaydre, President of the Genealogical Research Society of New Orleans, Webmaster of the German-Acadian Coast Historical & Genealogical Society

LOUISIANA LEGACY

History of the Daigle and Schexnayder Families

Edward O. Daigle

Foreword by Brian J. Costello, OT, OLJ

Louisiana Legacy: History of the Daigle and Schexnayder Families

For information, contact Neal Bertrand at Cypress Cove Publishing, (337) 224-6576.
www.CypressCovePublishing.com

Published by:

CYPRESS COVE PUBLISHING
PO Box 91195
Lafayette, LA 70509-1195

ISBN: 978-1-936707-40-9

Library of Congress Control Number: 2016946775

Edited by Neal Bertrand

Cover Design by eBell Design, Lafayette, La.

Interior Production by Jeremy Bertrand, Cypress Cove Publishing

DEDICATION

First and foremost, to my brother Vernon who first got me interested in the family history and to Monsignor Jules Daigle who contributed his vast knowledge of the historical family and instilled in me the importance of documenting this history.

To my children and grandchildren so you have an appreciation of where you came from and who you are. I hope in some small way the information contained within these pages helps to instill some pride in our State by having a better understanding of how unique Louisiana really is.

To my wife:
Susan (Mimi)

"You and I have lived and loved together
We have watched as the years continued changing

We have shared some good times
And we have shared some bad times

We have shared the joys of our children
And we have felt the anxiety of the unknown

We have felt the close times
And we have carried the burden of our distance

I want you to know the man you made me
And share, with me, our lives forever; together"
                                        Eddie

ACKNOWLEDGEMENTS

Norwood Marcy Lyons for the unpublished manuscript *Etienne Daigle,* provided by Jules Daigle.

Right Reverend Monsignor Jean Eyraud and Donald Millet for *A History of St. John the Baptist Parish.*

Brother Louis Welker, FSC, Christian Brothers, Lafayette for the Eulogy for Brother Gabriel Daigle (Armand).

Florence Daigle Perkins, President of the Association de la Famille Daigle, *The Eagles Wings.*

Carol Ann Aucoin, *Cajuns, A Culture.*

Michael Schexnayder, LSU, Schexnayder Family Data, Mike Schexnayder, CPA, *Schexnayder History.* Jean-Pierre, Descendant of Andre Daigle dit Lallemand, Quebec, Canada.

Austrian Government, Association of Daigle dit Lallemand, New France, Montreal, Canada.

Halpert's Family, *The World Book of Daigles.*

W. E. Butler, *Down Among the Sugar Cane.*

Agnes Foreman, *Zerangue, Zeringue, Zyrangue and Allied Families.*

Joy Donalson McGraw, *Building the Levees.*

Elton J. Oubre, *Vacherie,* St. James Parish History.

Louisiana Secretary of State, (Internet) *Louisiana Under Ten Flags.*

Gerald Keller, Ph.D., *Precious Gems from Faded Memories,* History of St. John the Baptist Parish. Carl Levet Family, *San Francisco Plantation.*

Carl Monica, Garyville Hotel & Library.

Monsignor Jules Daigle, *Dictionary of the Cajun Language* and associated unpublished manuscripts and letters.

Warren Perrin and Sam Broussard, Acadian and Cajun history.

Jay Schexnaydre, President of the Genealogical Research Society of New Orleans, Webmaster of the German-Acadian Coast Historical & Genealogical Society

Special thanks to Jay Schexnaydre for his historical contributions of the Schexnayder family

Warren Perrin and Sam Broussard for historical contributions of the *Acadians & Cajuns.*

Every attempt has been made to give proper credit to those individuals who have contributed interviews, photographs and family histories, and to those whose previous research has been reviewed by the author.

EDITOR'S NOTE:

The reader may notice a few instances where there appears to be duplicate content, and there is some, due to the fact that they are quoted from different sources.

CONTENTS

FOREWORD

In *Louisiana Legacy,* Mr. Eddie Daigle presents a scholarly yet lively, heart-warming and inspiring chronicle of two of the state's largest and best-known families, Daigle and Schexnayder, and their near relations. These two extended families, both Belgian in origin as evident from Mr. Daigle's painstaking research, have been prominent for nearly three centuries in Louisiana agriculture, education, lay and consecrated religious life. Recent generations have continued in the paths of their ancestors while adding their own invaluable contributions in the realms of business, technology, sports and the arts.

Through changes in government from a colonial French and later Spanish possession to Americanization, and surmounting such challenges as floods, epidemics, warfare and general changes in modern society, the Daigles, Schexnayders and relations have thrived and survived as a true reflection, indeed a microcosm, of Louisiana culture in all of its rich diversity. Gallant leaders in the development of New France, hearty German settlers, pious Acadian French exiles and other courageous pioneers all bestowed their genetic heritage, physical and spiritual strengths and individual cultural gifts to the making of the Daigle-Schexnayder family.

Mr. Daigle, having personally grown and matured through a period of exponential changes in his home state, the nation and the world, beautifully bridges the fondly recalled era of his grandparents, their generation and their precious legacy of oral tradition, through his own formative years and into the 21st century world of his cherished children and grandchildren.

A man of many talents and achievements and a true Christian Louisiana *gentilhomme*, Mr. Daigle eloquently presents the history of his antecedents in a scholarly yet easy-to-digest and lively style. Admirably, he combines primary documentary evidence and familial oral history and weaves it into the history of the state, clearly demonstrating how his ancestors helped form a truly unique American community and culture while responding to the transformations wrought by historical events. The text is supplemented by a wealth of vintage photographs as well as other imagery.

Privileged to have visited with Mr. Daigle and having read his manuscript in process, I heartily commend him for his admirable work and recommend *Louisiana Legacy* to any reader interested in the genealogy of the Daigle and Schexnayder families, their place in time and community, and the history and culture of Louisiana in all its rich diversity.

Brian J. Costello, OT, OLJ
New Roads, Louisiana

INTRODUCTION

Before the Acadians arrived in Louisiana, the cultural base of the people we know today as Cajuns was already established.

Frenchmen, Germans, and Spaniards had already arrived, and together with the indigenous natives and the Caribbean and Haitian Blacks formed a mixture known today as Creoles, Mulattos, Maris, and Sabines, which became a roux that when mixed with the Acadians formed the unique Louisiana culture.

Louisiana Legacy is intended to be in part a history lesson of Louisiana, which turns out to contain the basic history of our family. My intention was to create a document which could be utilized by any or all of our families' children who might desire to continue the genealogy for their own families while providing for them a sense of Louisiana history.

I grew up loving Louisiana, and even with our colorful past and politicians we are not so proud of, Louisiana is where I want to be. I hope, in a very small way, that this book imparts a sense of history of both our state and our family. I think it is incredible – and a stroke of fate – that two distinctly different families originated from the same foreign soil 330 years ago and managed, by different routes, to end up living close to each other in a new world only to part from each other for 80 years, and then end up with two members marrying to join these two families together. God may have had a plan all along. By any stretch of the imagination, this is an incredible twist of fate.

French Canadian lines of the modern Daigle Family: Proulx, Robidoux, Croteau, Balanger, Roman, Latiolais, Bergeron, Landry, Dupuis, Leger.

Note: The spelling of many names throughout the history of Louisiana have changed over the years, especially for the early settlers of Louisiana.

Acadian Journal, T. Hebert, 1997

Unfortunately, I could not find a link to the French/German lines of the Schexnayders except roughly twelve different spellings of the name Schexnayder. The modern names of Hymel, Waguespack, Melancon, and Zeringue are closely linked.

Note: Schexnayder, Schexnaydre, Sexchneyder, Sexnaidre, Snydre, Sixtailleur, Seckshneyder, Secxnauder, Scheixneydre, Chisnaitre, Cheixnaydre, Hexnaider are all spellings used at some time or another in Louisiana.

The Daigles and the Schexnayders were among the first pioneers in Louisiana, both appearing in the early 1700s. The history of Louisiana is not complete without the mention of these two families from their early days on the German Coast to the founding of Church Point, and on to the modern day families.

I have attempted to be as factual as possible, and as you will see there are circular references when possible which may appear as repeated information. The idea, as stated earlier, was to create a foundation for any family member who wished to continue the genealogy with their own family. With this book they can easily do so, picking up from their parents and discarding my personal family information.

SCHEXNAYDER & DAIGLE

Daigle / Schexnayder Family History

Background

In 1545, the Catholic Church made the use of a saint's name mandatory for baptism. Prior to this time only single names were predominant with only about twenty to thirty first names used. In the early 1600s the Protestants rejected anything associated with Catholicism and began to use names from the Old Testament.

Sicut Quercus

"As The Oak"

Coat of Arms of Jean Daigle

This Coat of Arms is the one that Father Jules Daigle says is the Coat more closely linked to our ancestry. The Jean Daigle Association, both here in Louisiana and in Quebec, Canada says this is the coat of arms from the Jean Daigle family. The two Coat of Arms have similar colors but distinctly different shields.

The second Daigle Coat of Arms, for the Olivier Daigle family is a black background with a gold eagle holding in its claws, arrows, covered by a silver armor head shield.

The coat of arms was woven into cloth and worn by the owner as everyday clothes, but mostly for ceremonial or actual battle use. Historically a Coat of Arms implies the owner achieved some notable feat. The colors and characters of the coat implied certain traits or historical facts. The colors, such as on the Daigle Coat of Arms, silver represents serenity and nobility and the blue represents loyalty and splendor.

Olivier Daigle Family Coat of Arms

The bearing of a coat of arms was restricted to the first son. Younger sons may use a version of their father's Arms, but the rules of heraldry say they must have had some change. If the bearer of a Coat of Arms (called an Armiger) dies without male heirs, his daughter may combine her father's Arms with that of her husband. In the modern world there are approximately one million surnames in use with less than 75,000 of these names being associated with a Coat of Arms.(1)

There is a third coat of arms (Jean Daigle) which displays the royal blue background with a dove holding an olive branch in its beak, with a soaring eagle over it. I did not display this coat of arms since I could not find any direct collaborative link to it even though the colors and eagle are present. It may have been a later coat of arms created by a younger son. *World Book of Daigles No. 06154*

Between the two more prominent Daigle coats of arms, the Jean Daigle coat of arms (*As the Oak*) is the one that Father Jules Daigle says is more closely linked to our ancestry, and the Jean Daigle Association, both here in Louisiana and in Quebec, agrees. The second Daigle arms, that of Olivier Daigle, has a black background behind a gold eagle holding arrows in its claws and is covered by a silver armor head shield. A silver upper third, charged with a sleeve hole, is also charged with a soaring eagle. The two arms have similar colors but distinctly different shields. The third as listed in the World Book of Daigles is similar to the first Jean Daigle coat of arms, in that, it represents peace but with a soaring eagle as protection.

The Daigles and Schexnayders both arrive in Louisiana about the same time, the Daigles 1717 – 1720, the Schexnayders 1721.

Note (1): Societe Francaise d'Heraldique et de Sigillographie, 113 Rue de Courcelles, Paris 17, France.

Note (2): Association de la Famille Daigle

French Beginnings 1682-1766

On April 9, 1682, Rene-Robert Cavelier, Sieur de la Salle planted the cross on Louisiana soil and erected a plaque with the French fleur-de-lis. He claimed the lower Mississippi Valley in the name of God and the French king. The Catholic colony that developed, with its center in New Orleans after 1718, quickly became one of North America's most culturally and ethnically diverse cities, with residents from Europe, Africa, the Caribbean and North American colonies such as Martinique and Canada, as well as a small number of Native Americans. The first Acadians arrived in the 1760s, forty years after the first Daigles and Schexnayders. The Louisiana colony formed a distant part of the Diocese of Quebec.

These are the colony's pioneer parishes and the years they were established:

Old Biloxi (Ocean Springs, Mississippi), 1699
Mobile in Alabama, 1703
Natchez in Mississippi, 1716
Robeline, 1717
New Orleans - St. Louis Church, 1720
La Balize near the mouth of the Mississippi River, 1722
The German Coast (later St. Charles in Destrehan), 1723
Pointe Coupee, 1728
Natchitoches, 1728
Chapitoulas (Metairie), 1729

The last seven are all in Louisiana.

In 1727, Ursuline nuns from France arrived in New Orleans to take charge of the Royal Hospital and to provide education for the colony's girls and women. They immediately began instructing African and Native American girls as well as the daughters of European settlers. Their school remains the oldest Catholic school for females in the United States.

At the end of the French period, more than a half dozen permanent settlements had been established in the lower Mississippi Valley. Already, a third generation of native-born Louisianans – Creoles – were appearing, particularly outside of New Orleans in lower Southeast Louisiana. Today, many of these Creoles are referred to by the pejorative name Sabines, a name for the mix of African American, Caucasian (French & Spanish), and Native American. Even today there are communities in Southeast Louisiana whose inhabitants are at times referred to by this name.

Louisiana Under 10 Flags

LOUISIANA HISTORY UNDER 10 FLAGS

1519 Alonso Alvarez de Pineda led an expedition along the northern shore of the Gulf of Mexico and discovered the mouth of a great river which may have been the Mississippi.

1542 The Spanish adventurer Hernando de Soto died on the shores of the Mississippi River near present-day Memphis while exploring the southeastern United States. Each year the Mississippi, an Ojibwa Indian word meaning "big

river" carries 400,000,000 tons of sediment into the Gulf of Mexico and discharges more water than all European rivers combined.

1682 The French explorer Sieur de La Salle, the first to descend the Mississippi to its mouth, took possession "of the country known as Louisiana," and named it for the reigning monarch of France, Louis XIV.

1714 Louis Juchereau de St. Denis founded Fort St. Jean Baptiste, present-day Natchitoches, the first permanent settlement in Louisiana.

1717-31 Louisiana experienced a surge of growth and development as a colony of the Company of the West and, after 1719, its successor the Company of the Indies. The Company of the West was an elaborate colonization scheme of the Scotsman John Law, endorsed by the French government, which wreaked havoc on the entire economy of France.

1718 Sieur de Bienville began building New Orleans as a company town for the Company of the West. By 1721 New Orleans had a population of more than 370 people, including 147 male colonists, 65 female colonists, 38 children, 28 servants, 73 slaves and 21 Indians.

1762 By the secret Treaty of Fontainebleau, France ceded its unprofitable and remote territories west of the Mississippi and the Isle of Orleans to Spain. It was 23 months later before the colonists in Louisiana learned they were no longer French subjects. Voltaire lamented the loss of Louisiana, saying that he could not conceive how Frenchmen could abandon "the most beautiful climate of the earth, from which one may have tobacco, silk, indigo, a thousand useful products." The average annual winter temperature for the state is 50.7 degrees, for the summer it is 82 degrees. Average annual rainfall is 55.45 inches.

1763 By the Peace Treaty of Paris, Great Britain acquired from France its Louisiana territory east of the Mississippi and north of the Isle of Orleans. Spain ceded to Britain its territories of East and

West Florida. Baton Rouge was fortified by the British and called New Richmond.

1788 The first Saint Louis church, completed in 1727, was destroyed by the fire of 1788 which destroyed four-fifths of New Orleans. When the city and church were rebuilt, the architecture was of Spanish rather than French style. In 1793, Louisiana and the two Floridas were formed into a new diocese and their headquarters was moved from Havana, Cuba to New Orleans. One year later, St. Louis church was dedicated as a cathedral. It underwent extensive renovations in 1850 and 1881.

1769 Spanish Governor Alejandro O'Reilly finally established firm control of Louisiana for Spain. O'Reilly divided the province into 12 administrative districts called

posts and 22 ecclesiastical parishes. The system of posts died with the end of Spanish rule, but parishes ultimately persisted as the primary county-level administrative unit under territorial and state governments.

1779 War broke out between Spain and Britain; Spanish Governor Bernardo de Galvez conducted a surprise attack on the British fort at Baton Rouge and captured the outpost. As a result of this victory, the West Florida Parishes were returned to Spanish rule.

1800 Spain officially returned the Louisiana territory West of the Mississippi to France by the secret Treaty of San Ildefonso to avoid the continued deficits the colony caused and the growing possibility that Spain might have to fight the restless Americans to retain control of the lands. (France did not actually take control until November 1803.)

1803 The United States purchased from Napoleon the territory of Louisiana for $15,000,000. Upon concluding the purchase, Robert Livingston, America's Minister to France, said of the transfer, "We have lived long, but this is the noblest work of our whole lives ... From this day the United States will take their place among the powers of the first rank ... The instruments which we have just signed will cause no tears to be shed; they prepare ages of happiness for innumerable generations of human creatures."

1808 The first public schools in the state were established in Pointe Coupee Parish.

1810 The American citizens of Spain's West Florida territory, who had dramatically increased in

number, took control of the Spanish government there and declared the territory a republic. The republic comprised the area of present-day Louisiana known as the Florida Parishes.

1812 Louisiana formally became the 18th state to join the union. William Charles Cole Claiborne was elected its first governor. The New Orleans, the first steamboat to navigate the Mississippi, arrived at New Orleans from Pittsburgh beginning the golden era of the steamboat.

1815 Andrew Jackson defeated the British at the Battle of New Orleans and saved control of the lower Mississippi for the United States. The British troops numbered about 8,000 to Jackson's 4,000 defenders.

From Louisiana Secretary of State Web Site

The Spanish Interlude 1766-1803

Louisiana became a Spanish colony in the 1760s. Church jurisdiction was transferred to the Diocese of Santiago de Cuba and later Havana. In 1793, the vast Diocese of Louisiana and the Floridas was created; the diocese stretched from Key West Florida, situated below the American colonies, to west of the Mississippi River and on up into Canada. Luis Penalver y Cardenas, a native of Havana, was named by the King of Spain as the first bishop. He arrived in New Orleans in 1795.

Church-state relations during the Spanish period were governed by the *patronato real*. The king had the right to establish dioceses, to nominate bishops, and to authorize missionaries to serve in the colony. In turn, the crown purchased and erected churches and schools, paid clergy, religious, and sacristan salaries, and even enforced Church laws such as Sunday observance. New Catholic parishes continued to be established, including St. John the Baptist Parish in Edgard (1772) and St. Bernard Parish below New Orleans (1787).

Louisianans, led by Governor Bernardo de Galvez, joined the Anglo-American colonists in their War for Independence from England. The British were defeated in a series of encounters at Manchac, Baton Rouge, Mobile and finally, in 1781, in Pensacola.

In 1788, New Orleans experienced the first of two devastating fires. St. Louis Church was destroyed in the conflagration. A new church was completed and put in use in 1794, thanks to the generous donation of Don Andres Almonester y Roxas.

By 1800, New Orleans was one of North America's most cosmopolitan cities. Of the 724 children and adults baptized at St. Louis Cathedral that year, 52% were slaves, 31% were whites, and 17% were free persons of color.

The native-born population was increased by natives of France, Spain, the Canary Islands, Cuba, Mexico, Bohemia, Italy, Canada, Scotland, Jamaica, Santo Domingo, Spanish Morocco, Puerto Rico, Martinique, Flanders, Ireland, and the African continent.

In 1801, Bishop Penalver was named the Archbishop of Guatemala. His departure soon left a void in ecclesiastical authority. The Louisiana Purchase two years later changed the direction of Louisiana Catholicism.

By this time the families of Daigle (1718) and Schexnayder (1721) were well established with the French Canadian Daigles (1760 / 1780) and Schexnayders (direct from Belgium) arriving in 1721. The Acadian Daigles arrived in Louisiana between 1760 and 1777. A second group arrived in 1780s. The Jean Daigle family had founded Church Point and had moved on to Opelousas before the Grand Derangement in 1755.

Societes de Genealogie Canadienne - Francaise Louisiana Secretary of State

Daigle / D'Aigle

Where did the Daigles come from and how did they end up in Louisiana? Some researchers say they came from a town in France called, Aigre, which was about 32 miles northwest of Angouleme; others claim the D'Aigles were peasants who actually had no last name and assumed the name of the town they were from when they migrated. However, records exist that clearly indicate a lineage from Jacques D'Aigle, born in 1591 in Brussels, Belgium and married to Armelle Jouet in 1616, as the progenitor of our direct line of ancestry. His descendant, Jean D'Aigle, is the ancestor who was recruited to New France (Canada) and arrived there in September 1668 as a sailor.

The Daigle family in Louisiana consists of both Acadians and French Canadians. The Acadian Daigles were deported by the British from Nova Scotia in 1755 to France before finding their way to Louisiana. The Canadian Daigles came to Louisiana in 1717 when Etienne (Marlborough) D'Aigle arrived in New Orleans from Charlesbourg. Etienne is my family's direct ancestor.

Etienne and his wife, Susanne D'Esperon or Despereau, lived in New Orleans until they obtained land on the west bank of the river, upstream from New Orleans in St. Charles Parish, where they and their descendants lived as farmers until the end of the eighteenth century. Etienne's wife is listed in the 1722 church records as Spanish/Creole, which probably means she was a mixture of Spanish, African American and Native American, or Islenos. The percentage of each is not given. Her surname is listed in the marriage records as D'Esperon, but in all other records found it is Despereau, which is predominantly Creole. It is possible that the Spanish version was used at the marriage, however, there were no negative connotations to being Creole at that time or now.

The D'Aigle family was well known in the parish with Etienne III being the most well known. His wife Marianne Tayon (Taillon) had four sons and four daughters. After the death of Etienne III in 1797, Marianne sold the family estate in 1803 and moved to the Opelousas area, where the sons began the very large branch of the Daigles of Southwest Louisiana. Etienne IV married Marie Doucet. Joseph (our direct ancestor) married Pelagie Doucet, and in 1803 they acquired land along the bank of the Plaquemine Brulée, which was the founding of Church Point, Louisiana in Acadia Parish. Alexander and wife Eloise Thibodeaux settled in St. Landry Parish.

For nearly a century the Church Point district remained the center of the Daigle family in southwest Louisiana, with some members moving to the Teche area near Breaux Bridge and Lafayette just before the start of the Civil War. (The Daigle family is still connected to land in Anse la Butte which Oscar Daigle and Edward used to cut fire wood, float down the Vermilion to Lafayette, then cut for fire wood) Attracted by large scale rice-farming, the Church Point family began to integrate into areas around Iota, Crowley, and Jennings in the 1880s.

While our direct ancestor is not Acadian, that is to say one who was expelled from Canada in the Grand Derangement beginning in 1755, two of

Etienne's brothers who had remained in Canada along with their families were in a group sent to Louisiana.

These were our cousins. This has caused much of the confusion as to when our family actually came to Louisiana. Many want to think of our family as Acadians. We are Cajuns culturally, yes, but not Acadians.

It should be noted that the Daigles in Louisiana are essentially divided into two families by ancestry and geography. That is to say that even today the Daigles from southwest Louisiana (west of the Atchafalaya River) are generally descended from Jean Daigle, while those in southeast Louisiana are generally from the Olivier Daigle ancestry. In Southwest Louisiana the name is pronounced *Day-gul*, while in Southeast Louisiana, it is pronounced *Daig*.

The Daigles of southeastern Louisiana are descendend from Etienne's two brothers who remained in Canada when he came to Louisiana. These Acadians were eventually expelled during the Grand Derangement and were shipped back to France, later making their way to Louisiana in 1785. In that year, eleven Daigle families, all Acadian refugees, disembarked in New Orleans.

One of the families remained in New Orleans while seven established homes along the Mississippi River between Manchac and Baton Rouge. The remaining three families settled along Bayou Lafourche. Among the Manchac / Baton Rouge group was the family of Olivier Daigle and his eight children, five sons and three daughters. From these eight siblings, Daigle families settled in the modern-day parishes of Lafourche, Assumption, West Baton Rouge, East Baton Rouge, and Ascension, and along Bayou Lafourche through Thibodaux and down to Houma.

The family of Jean-Mathurin, his wife Marie Levron and their four sons, migrated to the lower Teche to form another branch of the family. One son and daughter-in-law, Louis Maurice Daigle and his wife Anastasie Braud, settled in Attakapas where their descendants remain today, from Morgan City to New Iberia and the Marais Native American area south of Jeanerette.

Through the years many Daigles migrated back to New Orleans where they stayed, and 230 households of Daigles were listed in New Orleans before Hurricane Katrina hit.

From Monsignor Jules Daigle & The Association de la Famille Daigle

The death of our ancestor Jean is implied in a legal document dated March 14, 1700, which was drawn up for Charles Marette of L'Ange-Gardien, in the region of Beauport, Quebec, specifying the conditions of employment for one of Jean's sons, Etienne. In the document, it is written that Marie-Anne (Jean's wife) "gave her full consent... for seven years beginning at the feasts of the Pentecost the year before." This leads us to believe that Marie-Anne became a widow in May or June of 1699. No religious or civil document has been located concerning the death of Jean Daigle.

In July of 1703, Marie-Anne married Pierre Vilday, a native of Spain. Mr. Vilday was ordered to make an inventory of the goods belonging to the Daigle family and appoint a guardian for the children. At the same time, he rented the seigneury of Sieur Jacques Gourdeau, which was situated at the tip of L'îsle d'Orléans (Ste- Pétronille) and facing Quebec City. The list of items documented in the inventory from the Daigle home at Bourg-Royal (bed, plates, utensils, etc.) suggests that there were still two people residing there at the time, and that two sons, André and Jacques, continued living on the property until the fall of 1708 when creditors required the sale of the house in order to recover the unpaid taxes at the time of Jean's death.

On March 20, 1716, Pierre Vilday passed away. Following her husband's death, Marie-Anne settled in the lower part of Quebec City. She then marries for a third time, a Frenchman, Nicolas Cornières. This marriage is celebrated one month after her daughter Marie, married Louis Richard in July, 1716.

On December 17, 1742, Marie-Anne Perteau (her maiden name) died and was buried the same day. She was 76.

The descendants of Olivier Daigle lived in the Port Royal and Grand Pré areas of Nova Scotia. When the Grand Derangement started in 1755, some of them were deported to Virginia, which refused to take any Acadians. One group was then sent to England as prisoners of war for seven years before being released to France, where they spent 29 years. Another group ended up in Louisiana as part of the expelled Acadians.

The government of Spain needed people to come to Louisiana, which it owned. So in an agreement with France, the Olivier Daigle family and others were sent to Louisiana. They settled in

Bayou Lafourche, Houma, and some to the area around St. Gabriel and Baton Rouge. They are all descended from the same family.

Today there are Daigles in all 50 states, Canada, Belgium, Austria, and France. In late November 2007, while I was in Belgium on business, I met several people who not only recognized the name Daigle but were also quick to point out to me or ask if I knew that the name meant "Of the Eagles." This meaning of the name has also contributed greatly to speculation that the family had come from a mountain region of Austria. This is possible, as there are records that show D'Aigles in the area of Austria, marriage records in particular.

Monsignor Jules Daigle did point out that families moved a great deal to avoid religious persecution, and sometimes were split. It could well be that the early, pre-1590 D'Aigle name originated from the mountains of Austria and moved to Belgium to avoid the persecution. This would follow the movement of the original Daigles from Austria and Switzerland into Belgium in the early 1500s. The distance between Austria and Belgium is not great, and family marriage records indicate travel between the two countries.

Daigle Louisiana Descendants

We don't exactly know the circumstances, but we find Etienne in Louisiana, first by his wedding to Suzanne Despereau in 1722, and then in 1724 "à la Côte des Allemands," a region bordering the Mississippi River on both sides about 30 kilometers north of New Orleans. Marie-Josephe, his eldest daughter, married a Frenchman from Grenoble, Jacques Roman. Their descendants would form the Creole aristocracy of that era: wealthy landowners, judges, diplomats, and even a governor of Louisiana. Indeed, André-Bienvenu Roman, grandson of Marie-Josephe, was twice elected governor of Louisiana before the Civil War.

Roman's brother, Jacques-Télesphore, built Bonséjour for his wife, a sumptuous estate on the Mississippi River, southwest of New Orleans in Vacherie, now known as Oak Alley Plantation.

Alfred, son of André Bienvenu, was a judge, an author (biographer of General P.T. Beauregard), and book publisher. An herbarium of dried seaweeds dating from 1776 is part of the archives of the Daigle dit Lallemand's Association.

Two sons of Etienne "Marlborough," Etienne II and François, generated the Louisiana descendants (Etienne) and possibly the Arkansas descendants (François). On the other hand, Etienne III married Marie-Anne Taillon at Fort St. Louis in Missouri. This family came back to Louisiana before 1800 and settled in Opelousas in St. Landry Parish. Their descendants were among the first landowners of Church Point (Acadia Parish, Southwest of Opelousas), where we find most of Daigle *dit* Lallemand's families in Louisiana.

And speaking of Daigle *dit* Lallemand, it is interesting to note that the greatest advocate of the Cajun French language was Monsignor Jules Daigle (*dit* Lallemand). In 1984, he published his *Dictionary of Cajun Language*, and in 1992, *Cajun Self-Taught*, a study of the words and phrases of the language.

1720

On May 9, 1720, those who had become British subjects were offered free exercise of their religion, guarantee to their property, and their civil rights. Official notices were translated into French to be distributed (this continued from 1720 to 1755). An offer was made which allowed the French to leave, but not take any of their possessions with them. [Daigle, 51]

My assumption is that Etienne arrived in 1720 with the first wave allowed to leave, although there is speculation he arrived in 1717 or 1718.

- *Sociétés de Généalogie Canadienne-Française*

Family History
Daigle & Schexnayder

The Schexnayders think of themselves as German and the Daigles think of themselves as French. However, both families originated in the area around Brussels, Belgium. There does not appear to be any question that Simon Schexnayder, born 1681, was living in Brussels (Brabants) Belgium when Henry was born and that Henry arrived in Louisiana from Belgium. For the Schexnayder clan, Simon Schexnayder (Chegnider), married to Anne Marie Vesdray (Vasdray) in the very early 1700s, provides the earliest known history of the Schexnayders. Henri (Henry) Schexnayder, married to Anna Maria Magdelina Wiche, arrived in Louisiana in 1721 (or there abouts) and settled around Taft. (Note: early research by Jay Schexnayder places the Schexnayders settling around Luling.) Henry would have been about eleven or twelve years old if he did indeed arrive in 1721. There is confusion just who Henry married; Anna Maria Magdelina Wiche, from Stebbach, Germany or Anna Maria Magedlina Huisine. Current information says he married Anna Maria Magdelina Wiche.

"Inventory of the Community Property of the late Henri Albert Schexnayder and his second wife Marianne Edelmeier. Henri Albert died January 4, 1776 and Bellile orders an inventory of the property. The inventory was taken by unknown person of St. Charles Parish, in the presence of the widow, Marianne Edelmeier, Andre, Henri Albert and André Aidelmayre, son-in-law of the decedent, married to Catherine Schexnayder; and Josette and Julienne Schexnayder.

"His sons Jean-Baptiste and Adam and his daughter Catherine are not present. Schexnayder was married twice; first to Madelaine Wiche and second, to Marianne Edelmayer." [Document No. 214]

As you can see, confusion started early in the Schexnayder family and has carried through to today. They just have too many of them.

Note: Civil Records of St. Charles and St. John the Baptist Parishes and St. Charles Borromeo Church

For the Daigles, Jacques D'Aigle, born 1591 in Brussels, Belgium, married Armelle Jouett in 1616, in Belgium. George D'aigle, descendant of Jacques, was born in 1620 in Vienna, Austria, but was married in 1642 in Brussels, Belgium. This provides a solid link that the family was split, with some remaining and living in Austria. Jacques was the father of George whose son is Jean D'Aigle and Jean's son Etienne arrived in Louisiana in 1717 or 1720.

The point is that both families have historical ties to Belgium and Austria, and probably both are predominantly French. (Schexnayders may have been French speaking Germans) Following the names of the wives, it appears that most if not all of both families were of French origin up to the early 1900s. That being said, Gramma Schexnayder was a Zeringue of German origin. The Daigles arrived in Canada in 1674, and in 1720, Etienne D'Aigle arrived in New Orleans from Charlesburg, Canada, was married in New Orleans to Susanne D'Esperon, and died in La cote des Allemands, St. Charles

Parish. This was the area on the river between Lucy and Luling. The present day town of Des Allemands did not exist in the 1700s. This is the link to St. Charles Parish between the Schexnayders and Daigles. Both families lived and owned land in the vicinity of Taft.

The records show that the first move to Church Point – or Plaquemine Brulée, as it was known at the time – was by Etienne III, after his marriage to Marie Anne Taillon in St. Louis, Missouri in 1777. So between 1720 and 1777, the Daigles and Schexnayders are tied to St. Charles Parish and the area around Taft. It was in 1780 that the name D'Aigle in Louisiana was changed to Daigle.

The history and logs of the vessels which carried the Acadians to Louisiana from the Canadian expulsion are full of Daigles, and while originating from the same family, obviously the Canadian branch split with one group leaving long before the expulsion. It is for this reason there is confusion when following the history of Jean D'Aigle.

There were numerous accounts of the early Daigle family, but confusion exists on their origins and if they were French or German. The progenitor of our direct ancestry was Jacques D'Aigle, born in 1591 around Brussels, Belgium, which was predominately French but with a strong German influence.

Historical accounts through the Canadian records seem to start with Jean D'Aigle dit L'Allemand (the German) but Jean was the son of George D'Aigle and Marie Chavin. George was the son of Jacques and Armelle Jouett, names that are obviously French.

George was born in Vienne, Austria in 1620, and was married in 1642 to Marie Chavin in Brussels, Belgium. Jean D'Aigle was born in 1649 in La Rochelle, France and was married in 1685 in Quebec, Canada to Marie Anne Perteau or Perreteau, who hailed from Normandy, France. Records indicate that Jean D'Aigle dit L'Allemand (the German) arrived in Canada on February 2, 1674.

Father Jules Daigle indicated about this time that many of the people being expelled to Canada were criminals; not all, but most, and it is possible that Jean assumed another history to allow him to start a new life. This is strictly an assumption on my part from Monsignor Daigle's notes. I cannot find any records which ties Jean to being German. It is possible that he was assumed to be German since his father was born in Vienne, Austria, which at the time was predominantly French with a strong German influence. (Vienne is the French spelling of Vienna.)

It appears clear that the Daigles came to Louisiana via Canada while the Schexnayders came via France. There is a distinction between Acadians and French Canadians.

The names Marie Chavin, Jean's mother, and Armelle Jouett, his grandmother, are certainly not German. Jean's wife, who he married in Quebec, Canada was also not German; Marie Anne Perteau or Perreteau was born in Normandy, France in 1662. For the sake of local historical records we are direct descendants of Jean D'Aigle dit L'Allemand (the German).

Everyone is free to choose the ancestry which best fits your need for historical heritage.

The following is taken from the notes of Monsignor Jules Daigle's investigation while at the Vatican:

George D'Aigle, born in 1620 in a small Austrian village in the Austrian Alps, was known to be of French ancestry. He married Marie Chavin in Brussels, Belgium in 1642. During the 1500s, the Holy Roman Empire comprised present-day Germany, Austria, Switzerland, the Netherlands, and parts of France and Italy. In the early period of the 1500s, nobles in the German principalities of the Holy Roman Empire revolted in what was called the Knights War.

Religious wars continued into the seventeenth century. The Thirty Years War (1618 - 1648) began in Prague and quickly spread to the German principalities, Sweden, Denmark, and France. When peace was achieved, the Holy Roman Empire lost its German principalities, making it more of a dynastic Austrian State under Hapsburg rule than a Holy Roman Empire rule.

These conflicts and wars between Protestant and Catholics, and the final peace achieved, are what shaped modern Europe as we know it today. Austria was Catholic, and many Catholics throughout other regions fled to Austria. (Note: this fits with Jacques being born in Belgium yet having a son born in Austria, who then returns to

Belgium). France was the predominant power in the region at this time.

Since George D'Aigle and Marie Chavin were married in Brussels, Belgium in 1642, it has to be surmised that they travelled to Vienne from their village in the Alps between Vienne and Brussels (this is speculation). It is interesting to note that George – not known to be a German or a Frenchman – married a French girl, and that he used the family name D'Aigle. His father Jacques was also D'Aigle. There is further confusion when Jean D'Aigle is listed as Jean D'Eyme, a precursor of the family name Ayme/Aime of German descent.

However, it is clear that in no other records is there use of this name by Jean D'Aigle. There is also an account that Jean possibly was in prison at one time and used another name, but this is just another one of the many stories surrounding him. (Again, D'Eyme was originally a name of German ancestry, which may also account for his nickname, L'Allemand.)

Some accounts list seven children, others list six. Our direct ancestor is Etienne D'Aigle, born in Charlesbourg, Quebec February 2, 1693, the fourth or fifth child depending on whose account is being used. Etienne came to Louisiana in 1720 and married Spaniard Susanne D'Esperon of New Orleans in May of 1722. They first lived on the West Bank of the river, just west of the area around the Huey Long Bridge. (A previous account has them living in New Orleans before moving to the area of modern day Taft, St. Charles Parish) Etienne had the nickname "Marlborough," after the greatest

English general up to that time. There is confusion as to whether Etienne was a soldier or not. Some accounts list him as such and others do not.

The one thing that appears to be correct is the account of the family by Uncle Jules (see previous). During the Daigle Family reunion in Morgan City on August 14, 1999, it was evident that there is a great deal of confusion about the ancestry of the Daigle family in Louisiana, but absolutely no confusion that there were only two lines of ancestors: the French Canadian Daigles who emigrated before the Grand Derangement, and the Acadian Daigles who came to Louisiana from Nova Scotia via France during this expulsion.

Since both families used the name D'Aigle and both families used the term "people of the eagles," we may well have descended from a single D'Aigle family. During the Thirty Years War, many families were broken and dispersed to other areas of old Europe such as Brussels and Vienna.

It is documented that Etienne left two brothers in Canada when he left for Louisiana in 1720. These two brothers may have ended up in Louisiana during the Grand Derangement but would have been very old.

Note: *Etienne Daigle*, by Norwood Marcy Lyons is an unpublished manuscript of the Daigle family. While the majority of the data is correct, Jules had some problems with some parts of the document.

We know for sure that our direct ancestors, the French Canadian Daigles, came to Louisiana long before the Acadian branch that came to Louisiana via the deportation between 1755 and 1790.

Our ancestors arrived in Louisiana in 1720 (or possibly a few years earlier; see note below) and lived in St. Charles Parish, first close to New Orleans, and then in the area around Edgard or Wallace. Departing that area, Etienne III settled and founded what was known at the time as Plaquemine Brulée, now modern-day Church Point, Louisiana.

NOTE: The actual Louisiana arrival date of Etienne is in question as is the arrival date of Henri Schexnayder. The Daigle Family Association lists the date as 1717, and they indicate this date matches the marriage records in St. Louis Cathedral in New Orleans. The ship's log has not been found that lists Etienne, but there is a log entry that lists the name D'aigle. Other than this uncertainty, all other names, places, and dates match. However, the marriage records lists the date as 1722, and given it was May 9, 1720 that the French were allowed to leave Canada without belongings or penalty, 1720 is the more likely arrival date. The likely arrival date for Henri Schexnayder is 1721. These dates mean both the Daigle's and Schexnayder's arrived in Louisiana about the same time period.

The Daigle family lived and worked in the Church Point area until Joseph Daigle moved to Opelousas in the early 1800s. Francois Daigle moved from Opelousas to Lafayette around 1855. Gabriel Oscar Daigle was born in Lafayette on September 2, 1869, and died January 14, 1946 at the age of 77.

Gabriel married Gertrude Boudreaux on June 15, 1887, they had one child, Zeda, who is speculated to have died at birth, along with the mother,

Gertrude. The death of Zeda Daigle is speculation, death records could not be found for Zeda Daigle. The marriage only lasted a very short time, before the tragic deaths of the mother and daughter. However, only scant records of this period exist.

Later Gabriel married Eliza Landry (grandma). Eliza was born April 19, 1876, in Broussard, Louisiana and died August 8, 1958 at the age of 82. Gabriel and Eliza had seventeen children and whether Zeda was Regina of the marriage of Gabriel and Eliza or not is not relevant to the history of Gabriel and Eliza and their children.

The marriage of Gabriel and Eliza is listed as January 25, 1893. This means that in a span of 24 months from the date of their marriage, two children were born, Regina and Edward (December 27, 1894). There has always been a great deal of whispering that Regina was actually Zeda, the first child of Gabriel Oscar during his first marriage.

However, for this to be correct, Zeda (Regina) would have been five or six years old at the time of the marriage to Eliza. It would seem implausible that this could be hidden. Edward (my dad) never indicated that Regina was any other than his direct sibling.

Note: There are only slight and incomplete records of the years between 1887 – the recorded marriage of Gabriel to Gertrude Boudreaux and her subsequent recorded death shortly after – and Gabriel's 1893 recorded marriage to Eliza Landry. This lack of information has caused much speculation as to the correct position Regina held in the Daigle family. However, one thing is certain: Regina Daigle was either a sister or a stepsister to her 16 siblings.

Our Own Town

Daigle, Maine - In the late 1800s, about eight miles south of Fort Kent on the Caribou Road, a community became known as Daigle. Its name originated from first settler Vital Daigle, who came from Frenchville. In 1906 a new Catholic Parish called "Holy Family Parish" was established at Daigle.

The residents of Daigle donated the property to build the church and establish a cemetery. Chrysostome Daigle and his brother Denis donated the land where the church, rectory, granary, garage, and sexton's house was built, as well as the land for the cemetery.

Original Church   Monument
(The church no longer exists,
a monument in its place)

Construction of the first church was almost complete when a fire destroyed the entire building. It wasn't until 1910 that another church was completed. By the 1960s, even though the population of Daigle had remained the same, the Diocese removed the parish priest and Daigle became a mission. In November 2000, the church was leveled and a monument erected where the building had stood. The church no longer exists, but the cemetery remains as a final resting place for Daigle residents.

In 1998, while conducting a research project for General Dynamics, I was sent to the Navy Base in Bath, Maine, a very small town upstate. When I checked into the lone hotel, the girl taking the registration said "Daigle" as if she knew it, and I remarked that I found it strange that someone so far north could pronounce my name. She went on to tell me that most of her teachers in grade and high school were named Daigle and came from the town of Daigle, so to her, the name was common and to me a surprise.

Holy Family Parish, Daigle, Maine 1906 - 2000 Commemorating 94 Years of Ministry compiled by Laurel J. Daigle with the assistance of Parish Members, 2000.

The Family

Descendants of Jean D'Aigle dit L'Allemand met in Quebec, Canada July 14 through the 28th, 2001, with family members from Austria, Belgium, Canada, and several of the United States. The descendants of Jean D'Aigle number about 2,000. The land owned by Marie-Anne Perteau and that of her son André, Etienne's brother, along with the ancestral home (a one room log cabin) still exist, and satellite photographs tie directly to the records existing in New France (Charlesbourg, Canada).

I met Jean-Pierre Daigle at the Daigle Family Reunion in Morgan City and have corresponded with him on several occasions since. He has graciously provided a wealth of information on the history of the Daigle family and has contributed many stories to the *Eagle's Wings*, the newsletter of the Association de la Famille Daigle.

From Jean-Pierre Daigle, Quebec, Canada

The History of Jean Daigle dit L'Allemand by Jean-Pierre Daigle

Jean Daigle landed in New France as a recruit from the old continent in the fall of 1668. Marie de L'Incarnation described these new recruits as "a mixed breed; Portuguese, Germans, Dutch and some Moorish women." On December 6th of the same year, our ancestor renounced Luther's religion in favor of Catholicism. With the help of documents from that era, we are able to follow the main events that marked the life of Jean Daigle from 1673 on.

In the summer of 1673, Jean Daigle had to face justice according to the custom of Paris. His intervention in a quarrel between two drunken people, and his resistance to follow orders from police who were also trying to intervene, resulted in Jean being jailed for 15 days. He was fined 10 pounds and agreed to an order from the court preventing him, at risk of penalty of death, from ever being involved in a quarrel again.

In the following spring, Jean bought Pierre Ledoux's land, which was located in the Trait-Carre de Bourg-Royal, 3 miles north of Quebec City. He built his house on the flank of a hill and integrated quickly into community life. The one room log cabin is still there today. His closest neighbor was the Perteau family, and further south were the Bedard, Chalifour, Mignier, Paradis, Allard, and Boutet families.

In a document dated 1681, we learn that Jean was working as a sailor. His last will and testament dictated to notary Mr. Duquet and dated June 24, 1682, indicates that Jean is preparing for a long and perilous journey north. Jean dit L'Allemand was part of the crew of 29 sailors who travelled with Radisson and Des Grosielliers to Hudson Bay to regain control of the fur trade with the Indians. The ending of this mission was catastrophic for these two legendary merchants. English troops seized all the goods, including the boat, and required restitution for the benefit of the English merchants of New England.

November 5, 1685, Jean married the eldest daughter of the Perteau family, Marie-Anne. She was a native of France and was declared to be age 19 at their marriage.

The document also reveals Jean's European origin; "son of the late Georges D'Egme and Marie Chavin, who was still living and residing in Vienne, Austria." Jean is the first Austrian immigrant recorded in New France.

In 1689, Jean dit L'Allemand would accept an offer from Pierre Allemand to carry wood by boat where navigation is possible.

The first child of the Daigle-Perteau union died a few days after his birth in 1686. A second child, André, was born on November 2, 1688. Between the years of 1691 and 1698, Jacques, Etienne, Jean, Marie, and Jean-Baptiste were born.

Jean died March 14, 1700, as shown in the legal document drawn up for Charles Marette of L'Ange-Gardien, in the region of Beauport, specifying the conditions of employment for one of Jean's sons, Etienne.

End of the account by Jean-Pierre Daigle

Excavation of the Original Home of Jean
D'Aigle dit L'lallemand

Note: One has to be very careful in
following the ancestry, as each writer
sometimes uses a person's first name and
sometimes his second. As you can note in the
ancestry chart, there are several names that are
very common from one generation to another.

I have purposely included two accounts of
Jean Daigle dit L'Allemand to maintain the
perspective of two view points. Jean-Pierre, the
person who wrote this account, has lived his
entire life in the area of Canada where the
D'Aigles first settled. Some seemingly repeated
information is only to show the two
perspectives.

Daigles in the Civil War

From *The Daigle Legacy*, by Lynette LeBlanc Kleinpeter. Though the author is not on our side of the Daigle family, the book contains good references:

Joachim, Francois, Louis, Isidore, Joseph, Therance, Ursin, Alexis, Alcee, Eugene, Prudent, and many others joined at the onset of the war and served with the 4th Louisiana Infantry as Tirailleurs (sharpshooters). They fought at Fort Hudson, New Hope Church, Ezra Church, Atlanta, Nashville, and the siege of Jackson. At Hollow Tree Gap in Tennessee (*in which Daigle cousins are represented*), the Confederate forces were defeated and began a retreat to Louisiana, marching 127 miles without shoes or rations to Jonesboro. (*There were no Daigles in this march as far as I know.*) Only three brothers from the family of Joseph Isadore Daigle survived the war, but all three died a short time later. (*Joseph Isadore may be the son of Joseph Daigle who was the brother of Joseph Etienne Daigle.*)

Throughout the war, Joseph carried a Catholic prayer book in his vest pocket, and during a battle he was hit on the book, which saved his life. The book contains many hand written notations, one of which reads, "I am fighting under General Gibson, 1862, in Baton Rouge, where he was captured and became a prisoner of war." The book exists today and is in the hands of one of his descendants.

Monsignor Jules Oscar Daigle

On the speaking of French in Louisiana after the Civil War, he notes that all documents in Louisiana were published in both French and English, then in 1898, things began to change and documents were allowed to be published in French, but only in areas where French was the predominant language. In 1921, the Louisiana Constitution prohibited the teaching of French in public schools. In short time, children were punished for speaking French, and the shame that resulted and the influence created endured through the 1950s. Many parents were taught to feel shame for teaching their children French, and after the Second World War a person was considered ignorant or from the backwoods if he or she spoke French.

"Fortunately in the 1970s, a newfound appreciation emerged for a French heritage that gave natives a unique status in an increasingly homogeneous America. Monsignor Jules Daigle helped foster the revival by publishing a Cajun French dictionary."

Jules was ordained in the Vatican in 1925, and spent nine years there studying language history. He returned to Louisiana and delivered his sermons in French. Immediately he celebrated mass to overflow crowds. After returning to Welsh in 1930 as parish pastor, he was asked to return to Rome to study canon law, but fearing he would end up in an administrative position, he declined and asked to remain in Welsh as pastor. Over the years he turned down many opportunities to take over much larger parishes, always wanting to stay in Welsh. He remained there for 44 years.

"I loved the place. I loved the people, I married the people, I baptized their children and I have buried them all."

After 48 years as a priest, Jules retired in 1974 to begin a writing career. He spoke over a dozen languages, with primary emphasis on Latin, French, Italian, Spanish, Hebrew, Greek, and of course, Cajun.

Using $35,000 of his own money he published a 600-page Cajun Dictionary. It was a Louisiana bestseller and earned Jules over $200,000 in the first few years of publication alone, money that he donated to charities in southwest Louisiana.

Jules died in December 1997, but the results of his work have far-reaching effects that will live on into Louisiana's future. Even today, several hundred copies of his Dictionary are still sold annually. His work in the schools of southwest Louisiana and in adult education programs have insured that French will be taught in public schools, and that children and adults should be proud of their heritage.

"Jules Daigle's work sparked pride and realization that Louisiana's French heritage is important and worthy of preservation. It is a birthright of its native people."

Editorial in the Opelousas Daily World and New Iberia Press, January 16, 1998

Interview with Jules Daigle, May 29, 1993

Daigle said Louisiana's Legislative Act 22 of Dec. 27, 1968, establishing the Council for Development of French in Louisiana, has wasted millions of taxpayer dollars teaching the French language to schoolchildren instead of the "French language as it is found in the state of Louisiana."

"There's a difference between who the Cajun people are, what they are, what they think, and what the world represents them as being. The Acadians originated in the northwest corner of what is now France, a piece of land known as Amorica, east of the Bay of Biscay, north of the Loire River and west of the Seine River. On today's map Amorica is now the peninsula of Bretagne and Normandie and the fertile lands of Maine, Anjou and Orleanais.

"The Cajun people were Celtics that lived in Amorica during the great Ice Age. We can tell that because of the carvings on these great stones. In the last 15 years, we have found, on other megaliths, these same writings all over the eastern part of the United States."

Daigle maintains these Amorican Celts migrated from the Key of Biscay to the North American continent and settled in the Maritime Provinces of Newfoundland, New Brunswick, Nova Scotia and Prince Edward Island. In the early 17th century (1604) the French people began to colonize eastern Canada. Those located in the Maritimes (Acadie) were virtually cut off from both France and the main French settlements in the Saint Lawrence Valley.

Migration to Acadie (Canada) had nearly ceased by 1671, and two North American colonies developed in significantly different ways. Feuding began between the Canadian French and the New England British and in 1713 the French ceded Acadie to the British. Years later the Acadians were exiled.

"Today our schools are teaching our children that we are French that we are of French origin, that French is our culture. That is a lie foisted on our children. The Cajun language came into its own with the first Louisiana settlement.

"All the previous years we were forging our own language. We don't speak anything like the 17th century French. We use French, but like any other language Cajun borrows from other languages. The proof: there are more indigenous Cajun words in the Cajun language that there are French words.

"Every language had its own unique origin. Cajun is no exception. Cajun in not bad French, nor is it a dialect of foreign French. Cajun is a separate and distinct language in its own right, just as Italian, Spanish and French are distinct from each other as well as from their common origin, Latin.

"When the Italian people freed themselves from the domination of Roman aristocracy, they formed for themselves a new and different language from the Latin which had been imposed on them. The new language was more in keeping with their native character and their new found Christian culture. In doing this they did not "corrupt" the

Latin language. They updated and upgraded to suit their culture and some Latin words were kept, but the modern Italian is not Latin.

"Years later, the Cajun people did the same thing in respect to the old world French. The ultimate result was the Cajun language. A language made in Louisiana, by Louisianans, for Louisianans; so that language in Louisiana, Cajun is not a foreign language. It was not imported here; it is Louisiana's only native tongue."

End of Interview

Jules was chosen for recognition as our Outstanding Daigle on February 11, 1999 at the Acadian Village in Lafayette, and again recognized by the Association of Daigles in Morgan City, August 14, 1999, and the *Congres Mondial Acadien.*

Based on the research by Monsignor Daigle – which includes some assumptions –before arriving in Amorica it would appear that our early family moved up from a location in the Middle East, following the Egyptian trade routes through what is now Russia and continuing up into Finland, then into Denmark and the Netherlands. From there they apparently ended up in Croatia / Bosnia (Morica) then into Austria. In Austria and Switzerland, actual records exist of the family name D'Aigle. The trail from here is recorded, and moves to Normandy, Brittany (Amorica), and our direct ancestors are traced to Belgium in 1591. This journey apparently covered a span of several hundred years before finally reaching Belgium. There is a DNA project underway by the Daigle Family Association, and they are fairly certain the family origin can be traced or linked to North Africa several hundred years before the birth of Christ, as several links seem to appear in the mitochondrial DNA.

The Seven Daughters of Eve (2001) is a book by Bryan Sykes that presents the theory of Human mitochondrial genetics to a general audience. Sykes explains the principles of genetics and human evolution, the particularities of mitochondrial genetics, and analyses of ancient DNA to genetically link modern humans to prehistoric ancestors.

Following the developments of mitochondrial genetics, Sykes traces back human migrations, discusses the out of Africa theory, and refutes Heyerdahl's theory of the Peruvian origin of the Polynesians, which opposed the theory of their origin in Indonesia.

He also describes the use of mitochondrial DNA in identifying the remains of Czar Nicholas II, and in assessing the genetic makeup of modern Europe.

The title of the book comes from one of the principal achievements of mitochondrial genetics, which is the classification of all modern Europeans into seven groups, the mitochondrial haplogroups. Each haplogroup is defined by a set of characteristic mutations on the mitochondrial genome, and can be traced along a person's maternal line to a specific prehistoric woman. Sykes refers to these women as "clan mothers," though these women did not all live concurrently, and indeed some clan mothers are descended from others (although not maternally). All these women in turn shared a common maternal ancestor, the Mitochondrial Eve.

Armand Gabriel Daigle

"All life is a journey home; back to one's beginning and forward to one's end." *Gesundheit.* Brother Gabriel felt that while we are on this earth we are on a journey home, homeward bound pilgrims who cannot rest until we rest in God, our final destination. Gabriel was 92 when he died.

This understanding of a journey must have been taught to the family, as Dad would often speak of his sojourn through this world as just a short trip on the way home.

Armand was born on March 12, 1906. From a family of seventeen came five religious vocations, one to the priesthood, three to become sisters of Mount Carmel, and one to the Brotherhood. He made his first vows on August 15, 1923, after he had earned a B.A. in English from Manhattan College. His final profession of vows were taken at the Brothers Generalate in Lemberg Lez Hal, Belgium, where he became a teacher.

From 1933 to 1935 he studied French and Psychology at the University of Lille, France, where he earned a M.A. in Psychology. Gabriel went on to become Director/Principal at several Christian Brothers schools in the New Orleans-Santa Fe Province.

Discipline and strictness are two words that describe Brother Gabriel very well, but in all cases he was also very fair. Archival records show that 171 novices went through training with Brother Gabriel. As Director of novices, Gabriel had to give a spiritual conference every day, and he was often heard to say; "I hate giving conferences, and God has placed me in a position where I have to give one every day."

A Voyage to Nova Scotia in 1731

The following is a record written by Robert Hale during a trip to Nova Scotia in 1731. It is his sailor's log. Hale was a Colonel and a Representative of the Massachusetts House.

"On Monday, June 28 at 5 a.m. I rose and after breakfast walked about to see the place. There are about 15 to 20 houses or churches, one of which a flag is hung for evening prayers. To the other, a priest goes once a day only.

"The priest goes about during the day giving communion to the sick, dressed in his cassock. Dressed like a fool in petticoats, with a man after him with a bell in one hand ringing at every door and a lighted candle in the other."

"The landlord of the Tavern is where I lodged, a man of 52 years and the father of six children. At just about bedtime, we were surprised to see the family on their knees praying their devotions to the Almighty, while others nearby were drinking and smoking. This they do all of them, mentally but not all orally, every night and morning.

"The women here differ as much in their clothing, besides wearing wooden shoes. Their features and complexion, which is dark enough by living in the smoke in summer to defend themselves against the mosquitoes, and in winter against the cold. Their clothes look as if they were pitched onto them with a pitch fork, and their stocking are around their ankles. Their houses are but one room besides a cockloft, cellar and sometimes a closet.

Their bedrooms are made on the manner of a sailor's cabin, but boarded on all sides with a small hole big enough to crawl through, before which a curtain is drawn. They have two or three chairs and very little eating utensils. These French are a different people"

Taken from Les Archives Pere Clarence d'Entremont

List of Ships That Carried Daigles from France After Expulsion from Nova Scotia

L'Amitie - Left France in 1785 and arrived in New Orleans 11-8-1785. 17 families settled in Galveztown, 3 settled in Attakapas, 71 settled in Bayou Lafourche. 13 Daigles on board.

Le Bon Papa - Left France 5-10-1785, arrived in New Orleans 7-29-1785. 38 Families onboard, 37 of which settled in the area around St. Gabriel. Only one Daigle was onboard: Charles Daigle.

La Bergere - Left France 5-14-1785, arrived in New Orleans 7-15-1785. 73 Families on board; 28 were Daigles.

Le Beaumont - Left France 6-11-1785, arrived in New Orleans 8-19-1785. 178 people on board, 51 were Daigles. 41 of the Daigles settled in the area around Baton Rouge.

Le Saint Remi - Left France 6-27-1785, arrived in New Orleans 9-10-1785. 325 people on board, 5 were Daigles.

Interestingly, the dominant names of these people were Hebert, Robichaux, Dugas, Leveron,

Trahan, and the most dominant was Naquin. Ninety-five percent of this group settled in the Bayou Lafourche / Thibodaux / Houma area. These are the dominant names even today.

Le Ville d'Archangel - Left France 8-12-1785, arrived in New Orleans 12-3-1785. 299 people on board, 4 were Daigles. The ship ran aground at the mouth of the Mississippi and was stranded there for over 70 days. This group settled in the Thompson Creek area north of Baton Rouge.

Le Corshire - Left France 10-19-1785, arrived in New Orleans 12-17-1785. 80 people on board, 2 were Daigles.

Ships-Acadian-Cajun by Tim Hebert, 1998. Note: Most of the Daigles on these ships are of the Olivier Daigle family and have populated the Southeastern section of Louisiana. They would be cousins, and obviously today the Acadian Daigles have mixed with the French Daigles.

Notable Daigles From the Many Louisiana Families

Joseph Daigle was the great-grandson of Olivier Daigle. He was the son of Joseph Daigle and Madeleine Gautreau. In 1785, he led a band of Acadians from St. Anne to Madawaska, Maine. Here he erected the first Acadian Cross on the shores of the St. John River, near Madawaska, expressing the faith of the Acadian people in God and in the new land. The Acadian Cross is referred to as the "Landing Site," and is the symbol by which the arrival of the deported settlers is marked. At the foot of the cross is a place to kneel where they expressed their faith. Every year since it was erected, events are centered around the cross during the Acadian Festival. In 1980, the descendants of Joseph Daigle held a reunion at which the old cross was replaced with a new cross.

Paul Daigle - Musician. Wrote and produced several albums of Cajun music, has played at World Fairs, and has played with the legendary Michael Doucet and Tony Thibodeaux. Paul is considered one of the best accordion players in the Cajun music world and is the musician for the music written by Pierre Daigle for Paul and his band, Cajun Gold. Olivier Daigle family.

Theodule & Joseph Daigle - Two brothers of French Canadian descent who are considered the founders of Church Point, Louisiana. They were born on the Ave Maria Plantation on the outskirts of Opelousas. In 1843, the two brothers moved to the Plaquemine Brulée area, the original name of Church Point. In 1848, the Daigle brothers decided to find a chapel for the church property purchased by the Jesuits of Grand Coteau for $120.00. They procured the building, renovated it, and moved it to the property, where it became the first Catholic Church in Church Point. The brothers served in many political offices, and were credited with building schools. Reputed to be ambitious, they were prosperous and very generous with their time and money. During the Civil War, Theodule served with Bond's Company of the Louisiana Partisan Rangers.

Lauren Daigle - Christian songwriter and professional singer. Lauren was born in Lake Charles, Louisiana, and months later moved to Baton Rouge. She then relocated to Lafayette when she was seven. She attended LSU after high school, then moved to Nashville to pursue her songwriting and singing career. She was nominated for the 2016 Grammy Award for Best Contemporary Christian Music Album, and again in 2017 for Best Contemporary Christian Song. Daigle is currently nominated for three 2017 K-Love Awards: Artist of the Year, Female Artist of the Year, and Song of the Year. Growing up in a region steeped in blues, country, zydeco, and Cajun music, the inspiration of her culture gave her a unique framework for the worship music she created. But Daigle admits she almost pushed music to the back burner, unsure if it was her true calling until a devastating illness brought her young life into sharper focus. Lauren is the great, great, great, granddaughter of Theodule Daigle, one of the brothers that founded Church Point, Louisiana.

Pierre Varmon Daigle - Author of several books including *Tears, Love and Laughter: The Story of the Cajuns and Their Music*, and *Plow, Sword, and Prayers*, a historical novel based on the Cajuns in southwest Louisiana and southeastern Texas. *The Echo of Their Cries* is a novel about children's troubles in the classroom. In 1985 he turned his attention to music and wrote and produced several albums, including Paul Daigle and Cajun Gold. Olivier Daigle family.

Bern Daigle - A U.S. Marine pilot distinguished during WWII, the Korean War, and Viet Nam. One of the most decorated serviceman from Louisiana, he retired from the military as a Lt. Colonel only to join the CIA and serve another 8 years. During the Second World War he flew 95 combat missions into Germany. He earned 4 Distinguished Flying Crosses, 16 Air Medals, 3 Battle Stars, and the Philippine Campaign Battle Star. In 1950 he was recalled to active duty and flew combat missions into North Korea, where he was again awarded the Distinguished Flying Cross. In 1967 he was again called to active duty to fly missions in Vietnam and Laos, and the Laotian Government awarded him the Order of a Million Elephants, the White Parasol, and the grade of Knight by the King of Laos. He died in 1990. Andre Daigle family.

Father Jules Daigle - Instrumental in promoting and preserving the Cajun language in Louisiana, and published the Cajun Dictionary. Jules was ordained at the Vatican, where he studied language and history for many years. He spoke 14 languages.

Oneil Joseph Daigle - Entered the military in 1943 as a 2nd Lieutenant and became Adjutant General of the Louisiana National Guard. In 1998 he was inducted into the LSU Hall of Honor. Olivier Daigle family.

Gary Daigle - Producer, performer, and much sought after liturgist. Renowned in the field of liturgical music. Works collaboratively with the

Dameans, and was the Director of Music Ministry at the Franciscan Renewal Center in Scottsdale, Arizona. Currently writes liturgical music for most of the top Christian music groups around the world.

Steve Daigle - Currently the Dramatic Director of the Opera Theater Program at the Eastman School of Music in Rochester, NY. He has numerous opera productions to his credit as both a singer and director. He has also served on the faculty of the Oberlin Music Institute in Urbania, Italy. As a singer he has performed major rolls in many major opera productions. His most recent success was in performing an acclaimed performance of Leonard Bernstein's *Candide* at the Eastman School of Music.

Glenn Henri Daigle - Graduated from LSU in Political Science, joined the Navy in 1962, and was commissioned in 1963. In 1964, Glenn was assigned to the USS Kitty Hawk, flying reconnaissance missions over North Vietnam. He was shot down on December 22, 1965, and remained a POW until 1973. When he returned home, Glenn received a M.A. in Political Science from LSU. He was then assigned to the Pentagon, then transferred to the Unified Command in Hawaii, and later assigned to the Rapid Deployment Joint Task Force. In September of 1982 he retired from the military. Again returning to Louisiana, he enrolled in LSU Law School and received his J.D. in 1984. He is one of the most decorated military people in Louisiana history, receiving the Silver Star, the Legion of Merit (twice), Distinguished

Flying Cross, Bronze Star, Gold Star Combat Medal, POW Medal, Combat Action Medal, Navy Unit Commendation, Viet Nam Service Medal, and the Viet Nam Campaign Medal.

John Edward Daigle - Inducted into the Junior College Baseball Hall of Fame, April 2009. Johnny was the general manager and director of operations at USA Stadium in Millington, Tennessee. Johnny is the son of Vernon and Helen Daigle of Baton Rouge.

Valerie Daigle - Enlisted in the Women's Auxiliary Army Corps in 1943. She became a member of the 21st Regiment, Company Two, and was assigned to Fort Oglethorpe, Georgia. She was later moved to Fort Patrick Henry, Virginia, where she attained the rank of Corporal and was honorably discharged in January of 1946.

1591: EUROPE TO NORTH AMERICA

Today there are Daigles in all 50 states, Canada, Belgium, Austria, and France. In late November 2007, while I was in Belgium on business, I met several people who not only recognized the name Daigle but were also quick to point out to me or ask if I knew that the name meant "Of the Eagles." This meaning of the name has also contributed greatly to speculation that the family had come from a mountain region of Austria. This is possible, as there are records, of marriage in particular, that show D'Aigles in the area of Austria.

Where did the Daigles come from and how did they end up in Louisiana? Some researcher's say they came from a town in France named Aigre, others claim the D'Aigles were peasants who actually had no last name, and as was the custom, had assumed the name of the town they were from whenever they migrated.

Here is a good place to point out that there are two distinct branches of Daigle families in Louisiana. We have two main lines, an Acadian and a French Canadian line. The Acadian Daigles were brutally deported from Nova Scotia to France by the British in 1755 before finding their way to Louisiana. The event was called the *Grand Derangement*, an effort by the British Crown to make the Acadians disappear as a people, and there is disagreement among historians in considering the expulsion an act of genocide. The French Canadian Daigles came to Louisiana in 1717 (or 1720, depending on the document) when a certain Etienne D'Aigle arrived in New Orleans from Charlesbourg, Quebec. (Etienne is my family's direct ancestor.)

Since both families used the name D'Aigle, we may well have descended from a single D'Aigle family. During the Thirty Years War, many families were broken and dispersed to other areas of old Europe such as Belgium and Austria. This dispersion has caused much confusion. The one thing that appears to be correct is the account of the family by my Uncle Jules, Monsignor Jules Daigle.

Jules did point out that families moved a great deal to avoid religious persecution, and sometimes were split. It could well be that the early, pre-1590 bearers of the D'Aigle name originated from the mountains of Austria and moved to Belgium to avoid the persecution. This would follow the movement of the original Daigles from Austria and Switzerland into Belgium in the early 1500s. The distance between Austria and Belgium is not great, and marriage records indicate travel between the two countries.

So let's look at the records. The best we have for the Daigles begins in 1591.

Jacques D'Aigle was born in that year in Brussels, Belgium, and there he married Armelle Jouett in 1616. This provides a solid link that the family was split, with some remaining and living in

Austria. From here, the records improve with the birth of George and Marie's son Jean.

The following is taken from the notes of Monsignor Jules Daigle's investigation while at the Vatican:

"George D'Aigle, born in 1620 in a small Austrian village in the Austrian Alps, and was known to be of French ancestry. He married Marie Chavin in Brussels, Belgium in 1642. During the 1500s, the Holy Roman Empire comprised present-day Germany, Austria, Switzerland, the Netherlands, and parts of France and Italy. In the early period of the 1500s, nobles in the German principalities of the Holy Roman Empire revolted in what was called the Knights War.

"Religious wars continued into the seventeenth century. The Thirty Years War (1618-1648) began in Prague and quickly spread to the German principalities, Sweden, Denmark, and France. When peace was achieved, the Empire lost its German principalities, making it more of a dynastic Austrian State under Hapsburg rule than a Holy Roman Empire rule.

"These conflicts and wars between Protestant and Catholic, and the final peace achieved, are what shaped modern Europe as we know it today. Austria was Catholic, and many Catholics from other regions fled to Austria. France was the predominant power in the region at this time."

This fits with Jacques being born in Belgium yet having a son born in Austria, who then returns to Belgium.

Since George D'Aigle and Marie Chavin were married in Brussels in 1642, it has to be surmised that they travelled to Vienna from their village in the Alps between Vienna and Brussels (this is speculation). It is interesting to note that George – not known to be a German or a Frenchman – married a French girl, and that he used the family name D'Aigle. His father Jacques was also D'Aigle. There is further confusion when George's son Jean D'Aigle – the first of his line to cross the ocean to Canada – is listed in one record as Jean D'Eyme, a precursor of the family name Ayme/Aime of German descent. However, it is clear that in no other records is there use of this name by Jean D'Aigle. There is also an account that Jean possibly was in prison at one time and used another name, but this is just another one of the many stories surrounding him. (Again, D'Eyme was originally a name of German ancestry, which may also account for his nickname, "L'Allemand" – the German.)

The names Marie Chavin, Jean's mother, and Armelle Jouett, his grandmother, are certainly French, not German. Jean's wife, whom he married in Quebec, was also not German: Marie Anne Perteau, or Perroteau, was born in Normandy, France in 1662. In addition, I cannot find any records which ties Jean to being German. It is possible that he was assumed to be German since his father was born in Vienne, or Vienna, Austria, which at the time was predominantly French with a strong German influence.

For the sake of local historical records we are direct descendants of Jean D'Aigle dit L'Allemand. In the interest of completion, I will present you with conflicting accounts, in particular those concerning

Jean as well as the movement of two of his sons. Everyone is free to choose the ancestry which best fits your need for historical heritage.

JEAN L'ALLEMAND

Nothing is known about the circumstances of Jean's arrival in Canada in 1668 – in fact, even the date is in dispute. The thing to remember about this time was that most of the people being expelled to Canada were criminals; not all, but most, and it is possible that Jean assumed another history to allow him to start a new life. This is strictly an assumption on my part, but you will see below another account that presents Jean as being no stranger to conflict.

Descendants of Jean D'Aigle dit L'Allemand met in Quebec, Canada July 14 through 28, 2001, with family members from Austria, Belgium, Canada, and several of the United States. The descendants of Jean D'Aigle number about 2,000. The land owned by Marie-Anne Perteau and that of her son André, the brother of our ancestor Etienne, is tied by satellite photographs directly to the records existing in Charlesbourg. The ancestral home, a one room log cabin, still exists.

I met Jean-Pierre Daigle at the Daigle Family Reunion in Morgan City and have corresponded with him on several occasions since. He has graciously provided a wealth of information on the history of the Daigle family and has contributed many stories to the *Eagle's Wings*, the newsletter of the *Association de la Famille Daigle*.

One has to be very careful in following the ancestry, as a writer may sometimes use a person's first name and sometimes his second. As you can note in the ancestry chart, there are several names that are very common from one generation to another. Also another account lists the date of Jean's death to be August 26, 1699, only a little earlier than Jean-Pierre's date given. I have included another account of Jean Daigle to maintain the perspective of two view points. Jean-Pierre, the writer of this account, has lived his entire life in the area of Canada where the D'Aigles first settled.

Jean-Pierre Daigle, Quebec, Canada

JEAN II

The information below was taken from the Eagles Wings, Volume 2 Number 2, the newsletter of the Daigle Family. This information is in conflict with the genealogy of Monsignor Jules Daigle found in The Historical Family section. It appears to be Etienne III who may have first arrived in Church Point.

"The ancestor of the Daigles from the Prairie area of Church Point was Jean D'Aigle, who arrived in Canada from France in 1674. Jean was a soldier – or a sailor – and took part in a military expedition against the English in Hudson Bay in 1682. When he returned from the expedition he settled in Quebec, married, and became a farmer.

"The first French Canadian Daigle to arrive in Louisiana was Etienne Daigle, in 1717. He arrived in Opelousas about 1800. He fathered Joseph Daigle, who fathered Theodule and Joseph along with 14 other children. Theodule and Joseph are noted as the founders of Church Point. They settled in the Plaquemine Brulée area, as it was called at the time, later named Church Point.

"As more Catholics arrived in the area the Daigle brothers purchased a building to be used as the church, then donated the land for the first Catholic Church in Church Point."

JEAN'S DESCENDANTS: ETIENNE I, II, and III

The death of our ancestor Jean is implied in a legal document dated March 14, 1700, which was drawn up for Charles Marette of L'Ange-Gardien, in the region of Beauport, Quebec, specifying the conditions of employment for one of Jean's sons, Etienne. In the document, it is written that his wife Marie-Anne "gave her full consent... for seven years beginning at the feasts of the Pentecost the year before." This leads us to believe that Marie-Anne became a widow in May or June of 1699. No religious or civil document has been located concerning the death of Jean Daigle.

In July of 1703, Marie-Anne married Pierre Vilday, a native of Spain. Mr. Vilday was ordered to make an inventory of the goods belonging to the Daigle family and appoint a guardian for the children. At the same time he rented the seigneury of Sieur Jacques Gourdeau, which was situated at the tip of L'îsle d'Orléans (Ste- Pétronille) and facing

Quebec City. The list of items documented in the inventory from the Daigle home at Bourg-Royal (bed, plates, utensils, etc.) suggests that there were still two people residing there at the time, and that two sons continued living on the property until the fall of 1708 when creditors required the sale of the house in order to recover the unpaid taxes at the time of Jean's death.

On March 20, 1716, Pierre Vilday passed away. Following her husband's death, Marie-Anne settled in the lower part of Quebec City. She then married for a third time, a Frenchman, Nicolas Cornières. This marriage is celebrated one month after her daughter Marie married Louis Richard in July of 1716.

On December 17, 1742, Marie-Anne Perteau (her maiden name) died and was buried the same day. She was 76.

During the Daigle Family reunion in Morgan City on August 14, 1999, it was evident that there is a great deal of confusion about the ancestry of the Daigle family in Louisiana, but absolutely no confusion that there were only two lines of ancestors: the French Canadian Daigles, who emigrated before the *Grand Derangement*, and the Acadian Daigles, who came to Louisiana from Nova Scotia during this expulsion.

For Jean and Marie-Anne, some accounts list seven children, others list six – but one is our direct ancestor: Etienne D'Aigle, born in Charlesburg, Canada February 2, 1693, the fourth or fifth child depending on whose account is being used.

Etienne came to Louisiana in 1717 or 1720 – depending on the account –and married Susanne

D'Esperon (or Despereau) of New Orleans in May of 1722. They settled on the West Bank of the river, just west of the area around the Huey Long Bridge after living in New Orleans for a short time. Etienne had the nickname "Marlborough," after the greatest English general up to that time. There is confusion among the accounts as to whether Etienne had been a soldier or not.

Etienne and his wife Susanne lived in New Orleans until they obtained land on the west bank of the river and upstream from New Orleans in St. Charles Parish. They and their descendants lived there as farmers until the end of the eighteenth century. Etienne's wife is listed in the 1722 church records as Spanish/Creole, which probably means she was a mixture of Spanish, African American and Native American, or Islenos. The percentage of each is not given. Her surname is listed in the marriage records as D'Esperon, but in all other records found it is Despereau, which is predominantly Creole. It is possible that the Spanish version was used at the marriage, but there were no negative connotations to being Creole at that time or now.

According to *Société de Généalogie Canadienne-Française,* on May 9, 1720, those who had become British subjects were offered free exercise of their religion, guarantee to their property, and their civil rights. Official notices were translated into French to be distributed (this continued from 1720 to 1755). An offer was made which allowed the French to leave but not take any of their possessions with them.

My assumption is that Etienne arrived in 1720 with the first wave allowed to leave, although there is speculation he arrived in 1717 or 1718. Henri Albert Schexnayder arrived in Louisiana 1721.

We don't exactly know the circumstances, but we find Etienne in Louisiana first by his wedding to Suzanne Despereau in 1722, and then in 1724 "à la Côte des Allemands," a region bordering the Mississippi river on both sides about 30 kilometers north of New Orleans on the west bank of the river. This area is the area west of modern day Taft between Wallace and Luling.

Marie-Josephe, his eldest daughter, married a Frenchman from Grenoble, Jacques Roman. (Roman's brother, Jacques-Télesphore, built Bonséjour for his wife, a sumptuous estate on the Mississippi river in Vacherie, southwest of New Orleans.)

Two sons of Etienne "Marlborough," Etienne II and François, generated the Louisiana descendants (Etienne) and possibly the Arkansas descendants (François). On the other hand, Etienne III married Marie-Anne Taillon at Fort St. Louis in Missouri, and this family came back to Louisiana before 1800 to settle in Opelousas in St. Landry Parish. Their descendants were among the first landowners of Church Point (Acadia Parish, Southwest of Opelousas), where we find most of Daigle *dit* L'Allemand's descendants in Louisiana.

The Etienne D'Aigle family was well known in St. Charles Parish – and the family of Etienne II as well – but Etienne III was the most well known. He and his wife Marianne Tayon (Taillon) had four sons and four daughters. After the death of Etienne

III in 1796, Marianne sold the family estate in 1803 and moved to the Opelousas area, where the sons began the very large branch of the Daigles of Southwest Louisiana. Etienne IV married Marie Doucet. Their son Joseph Chevalier (our direct ancestor) married Pelagie Doucet, and in 1803 they acquired land along the bank of the Plaquemine Brulée, which was the founding of Church Point, Louisiana in Acadia Parish. Brother Alexander (born Magloire-Alexandre) and wife Eloise Thibodeaux settled in St. Landry Parish.

For nearly a century the Church Point district remained the center of the Daigle family in southwest Louisiana, with some members moving to the Teche area near Breaux Bridge and Lafayette just before the start of the Civil War. (The land owned today by the Daigle family in Anse la Butte is the original from this move.) Attracted by large scale rice farming, the Church Point area the family began to integrate into areas around Iota, Crowley, and Jennings in the 1880's. Movement of their descendants continued west to the present day, where Daigles are found in Calcasieu Parish and in southeastern Texas.

THE DAIGLE GENERATIONS

Genealogical research is only as good as the records that are kept. The main sources for establishing New World family lines are the church recordings of births, marriages, and deaths that mark the passages of our mortal existence. The fragility of early construction insured that these buildings were themselves mortal, and those that burned took their records with them. Other records were moved as a diocese or parish would expand or have its boundaries redrawn, and in the Old World entire populations would relocate and/or change the spelling of their names or their names entirely on the occasions of famine, or more often, the innumerable wars that punctuate human history. Confusion results, and the researcher is left with ships' logs, property sales, and other legal documents – paper trails as fragile as any wooden building – with which to trace a lineage.

I have profited from the work of the *Societes de Genealogie Canadienne-Francaise,* the Daigle Association of Louisiana and others as well as the research of Daigle relatives. I have also been advised by a Louisiana historian to stay close to the research of my own Uncle Jules, Monsignor Jules Daigle of Lafayette, a prolific man who spent many years on genealogy as well as authoring two books on the Cajun French language.

I have begun our family's line in 1591 with the birth of Jacque D'Aigle. In Generation 3 you will find my note on an "alternate" grandson, Jean D'Aigle, believed by some to be a direct ancestor. His existence was probably confined to Acadia (modern-day Nova Scotia), while the favored research points more to Jean "L'Allemand" D'Aigle of Quebec as being the father of our undisputed ancestor, Etienne D'Aigle, nicknamed "Marlborough" after the famous British general.

There is also some confusion as to the identity of one Olivier D'Aigle or Daigre, who may or may not have been closely related to our line early on, but whose coat of arms – with similarities to our own – survives to this day.

What is not in dispute is that although Daigles were exiled to Louisiana in the 1755 expulsion by the British (known as the *Grand Derangement*), our direct ancestor Etienne's arrival in Louisiana predates that event by several decades. So while we are certainly Cajuns culturally, technically we are not Acadians.

I present our family's lineage here with confidence in its correctness going back to Brussels, Belgium, with the birth of Jacque D'Aigle in 1591.

Generation 1

Jacques D'Aigle, born in Brussels, Belgium in 1591 and was married to Armelle Jouett in 1616 in Brussels, Belgium.

Children: George D'Aigle, born in Vienna, Austria in 1620.

Generation 2

George D'Aigle, born in Brussels, Belgium in 1620 and married Marie Chavin in Brussels in 1642.

Children: Jean D'Aigle, 1649 - 1699.

Generation 3

Jean D'Aigle dit L'Allemand was born in 1649 in La Rochelle, France and died August 26, 1699 in Hotel Dieu, Quebec, Canada. He married Marie Anne Perteau (or Perroteau) November 5, 1685 in Charlesbourg, Canada, the daughter of Etienne Perteau and Marguerite Sequin. Etienne Perteau was born in Normandy, France.

Children:

1 Jacques Daigle, died January 13, 1730 in Quebec, Canada. He married Catherine Aubier.

2 Jean Daigle

3 Jean Baptist Daigle

4 Andre Daigle born 1689, died April 27, 1727 in St. Antoine, Tilly, Canada.

5 **Etienne (Marlborough) Daigle**, born February 7, 1693 in Charlesbourg, Canada

6 Marie Daigle, born 1696 in Canada

Note: As stated, some research points to a different Jean D'Aigle or Daigre, born in 1643 in

Aigre, in the Poitou region of France. Almost all Acadians hail from this region.

In 1663, this Jean sailed from France to Acadia aboard the ship *LaPaix*. He married at Port Royal in 1666 to Marie Gaudet, the daughter of Denis Gaudet, who was born in France in 1625. Jean and Marie had 10 children between the years 1667 and 1687.

It is their descendants that some have traced back as the Acadian Daigles, who were included among the exiles in the expulsion that began in 1755. However, regardless of the confusion of these two Jeans, the direct ancestor of our bloodline, Jean's son Etienne, arrived in Louisiana long before the Acadian Exile. According to the best research I have – that of Uncle Jules – he was the son of Jean L'Allemand and Marie Anne Perteau (Perroteau, Proteau) of Charlesbourg, Quebec, and not Acadie. Other Daigles who may have been related had remained in Canada and were expelled with the other Acadians, thus some confusion as to whether we were part of the exile or not. The truth is that our direct ancestor, Etienne, was not.

Generation 4
Etienne (Marlborough) D'Aigle was born in Charlesbourg, Canada on February 7, 1693. He arrived in Louisiana in 1717 and married Susanne D'Esperon (Desperau) in May of 1722.

Children:

Etienne Daigle II, born 1725, died April 2, 1798 in New Orleans.

Marie Josephe Daigle, born 1725 in New Orleans. She married Jacques Roman on October 24, 1741 in St. Charles Borromeo Church, St. Charles Parish, Louisiana.

Francois Daigle, born November 6, 1729 in New Orleans, died December 13, 1744 in Destrehan, La.

Joseph Daigle, born May 12, 1733.

Francois Daigle, born 1735, died September 22, 1743.

Generation 5

Etienne D'Aigle II was born in 1725 and died in New Orleans on April 2, 1798. He married Angelique LaPrade in 1750 in St. Charles Parish, La.

Children:

Joseph Daigle, married Marie Josephe Duguet, February 26, 1782 in St. Francis Church, Pointe Coupee, La.

Alexis Daigle, died July 27, 1786.

Francois Daigle

Felicite Daigle, married Alexis Bertrand.

Francoise Daigle

Gertrude Daigle, born June 4, 1754, died September 28, 1787.

Cecile Daigle

Angelique Daigle, born April 10, 1751 in New Orleans. She married Pierre Loirot September 28, 1770 in Conrad, St. Charles Parish, La.

Etienne Daigle III, born August 8, 1752 in St. Charles Parish. Died December 13, 1796 in St. Charles Parish.

Andre Daigle, born June 4, 1754 in New Orleans.

Jean Daigle, born December 24, 1767.

Generation 6

Etienne D'Aigle III was born August 8, 1752 in St. Charles Parish. and died December 13, 1796 in Taft, St. Charles Parish, La. He married Marie Anne Taillon on August 5, 1777 in St. Louis, Missouri, daughter of Joseph Taillon and Marie Boisset.

Children:

Etienne D'Aigle, born 1779, died June 21, 1864 in Church Point. **Joseph Chevalier D'Aigle**, born 1780 in St. Charles Parish, and died July 21, 1864.

Magloire-Alexandre D'Aigle, born 1781 in St. Charles, Parish, and died October 4, 1840 in Opelousas. Married Eloise Thibodeau on November 24th, 1822.

Marie Gertrude D'Aigle, born 1787, died December 4, 1828 in New Orleans.

Marie Josephine D'Aigle, born November 6, 1788 in St. Landry Church, Opelousas, and died August 2, 1858 in Church Point, La. She married Lufroy Latiolais on February 13, 1811, in Opelousas.

Eugene D'Aigle, born 1792, died August 8, 1817 in Brulé, La. Eugene is the link to Baton Rouge-Pierre Part Daigles.

Marie Zelia D'Aigle, born 1794.

Marie Louise D'Aigle, born 1796. She married Jacques Dalbourg on October 27, 1835 in Opelousas.

Note: Following the family's locations, births, and deaths, there was a well documented link between this generation and St. Charles Parish early on, as well as a link to Plaquemine Brulé (Church Point) and Opelousas later on. The main point here is that there is documentation in St. Charles Parish placing the Daigles and Schexnayders in very close proximity to each other at the same point in time. I could not establish if they were actually on adjoining property, but according to the sale documents it appeared they were close.

From the St. Charles Parish Courthouse, No. 565 January 28, 1783: "Louis Falgoust declares, in the presence of Jacques and Etienne Daigle, that he has sold his farm to Joseph Bourgeois, 2 arpents wide by the customary depth, located 25 miles above New Orleans on the left bank of the river, bounded above by the property of Widow Roy and below by that of the vendee, for 260 piastres."

From the Catholic Register: "German Coast Daigles and Christian Grabert families were bear hunters and lived for a time in Arkansas on the White River, but Indian troubles forced them back to St. Charles Parish to settle. For years they traded with the Osages and Quapaws, trading bear oil, pork lard and salted pork."

From the St. Charles Parish Courthouse, Act No. 756 January 19, 1787: "Catherine Lepine, Widow Lambert, declared, in the presence of Etienne Daigle and Robert de la Villeneuve, that she gave power of attorney to her son, Louis Lambert (fils) to buy slaves with the proceeds from the sale of a house in New Orleans."

It is obvious from these records and others that the Daigles did locate in the area west of the current day Taft, St. Charles Parish, and lends credibility to the story of the Daigles and Schexnayders living next to each other in that area. It is apparent that the area along the west bank of the river from the St. John the Baptist Parish line East, the area of Wallace, Edgard, Killona, Taft, were in close proximity while Hahnville and Luling were to the East side of the parish.

Generation 7

Joseph Chevalier D'Aigle was born 1780, in St. Charles Parish and died July 21, 1864 in Opelousas, La. The family name changed from D'Aigle to Daigle around the time of Joseph's birth. His first marriage was to Pelagie Doucet, July 19, 1803 in Opelousas. (Pelagie was age 13 at the time of her marriage) His second marriage was to Josephine Fontenot, April 14, 1830 in Opelousas.
Children:
Joseph Etienne Daigle, born October 14, 1804, died February 20, 1844 in Opelousas.
Caroline Daigle, born July 24, 1805 in Opelousas, died 1902 in Opelousas.
Zephias Daigle
Joseph Daigle

Generation 8

Joseph Etienne Daigle was born October 14, 1804 and died February 20, 1844 in Opelousas. He married Lise Dupre on April 9, 1822 in Opelousas.

Children:

Joseph Ernest Daigle, born February 6, 1823 in Opelousas, died December 11, 1854 in Church Point.

Theodule Daigle, born October 1, 1824 in Opelousas, died November 21, 1907 in Church Point.

Francois Daigle, born April 26, 1826 in Opelousas, died April 4, 1874 in Lafayette.

Sosthene Daigle, born January 14, 1828 in Opelousas, died September 14, 1829 in Opelousas.

Marie Josephine Daigle, born November 21, 1829 in Opelousas. She married Antoine Guidry on June 11, 1844 in Grand Coteau, La.

Pelagie Daigle, born November 27, 1832 in Opelousas, died October 20, 1842 in Opelousas.

Zephyrin Daigle, born August 3, 1834 in Church Point, died April 7, 1923 in Church Point.

Therance Daigle, born February 12, 1836 in Church Point.

Marie Elisa Daigle, born April 9, 1838 in Grand Coteau, died January 6, 1897 in Church Point. She first married Alfred Bacon, June 22, 1852 in Grand Coteau, and her second marriage was to Lastie Fruge, on February 28, 1857 in Opelousas.

Marie Caroline Daigle, born June 18, 1839 Grand Coteau, died November 11, 1842 in Grand Coteau.

Celeste Marie Daigle, born October 23, 1841 Grand Coteau, married Simon Boudreau May 24, 1866 in Lafayette.

Generation 9

Francois Daigle, born April 26, 1826 in Opelousas, and died April 4, 1874 in Lafayette. He married Leocade Boudreau June 27, 1850 in Lafayette. Leocade was born May 20, 1833 in Ville Platte. Francois was a Louisiana State Senator at age 46.

Children:

Francois Daigle, born December 20, 1867 in Lafayette.

Gabriel Oscar Daigle, born Sept 2, 1869 in Lafayette. This is Grandpa Daigle.

Joseph Julius Daigle, born Nov 29, 1870 in Lafayette.

Flavius Daigle, born January 6, 1873 in Lafayette.

Gaston Idal Daigle, born June 25, 1874 in Lafayette. He married Louisa Broussard May 5, 1905 in Lafayette.

The story of the Daigles at this point in time seems to have been romanticized from a letter written to Velma Daigle by Quorum Daigle, who was represented by her, probably in error, as the son of Francois and Leocade. As noted above, Francois and Leocade had six children, one of which is Grandpa Daigle. It seems the author, Quorum, somehow got the names of the children confused, mixed up, or just plain wrong at this point. You will also note that Grandpa is listed as

Gabriel Oscar in the genealogy, while in other documents, including the letter from Quorum, he is listed as simply Oscar Daigle. My observation is that Quorum is actually a descendant of Olivier Daigle, who in some documents is described as the brother of Jean D'Aigle dit L'Allemand of Generation 3. Quorum does not show up in the direct linage. Later in Generation 10, take note of the actual Historical Records of Lafayette Parish, St. John Catholic Church.

Generation 10

Gabriel Oscar Daigle was born September 2, 1869 in Lafayette. He died there January 4, 1946. He first married Gertrude Boudreaux on June 15, 1887, in Lafayette. They had one child, Zeda, and she and Gertrude may have both died in childbirth. His second marriage was to Eliza Landry (Grandma Daigle) on January 25, 1893 in Lafayette. Eliza was the daughter of Charles Landry and Marie Chaisson of Broussard, La.

Grandma Daigle
Born April 15, 1876
Died August 8, 1958

Children:

1. Regina, born October 14, 1893 in Lafayette. First married to Darcey, and a second marriage to Joseph Chargois. Vivian Darcey, the daughter from the first marriage, lived with Regina and Joseph and their son John Chargois.
2. **Edward Oscar**, born December 27, 1894 in Lafayette. Married to Leah Schexnayer on September 20, 1920.
3. Leocade (Sister Veronica), born July 21, 1896, in Lafayette.
4. Gabriel Charles, born November 8, 1897 in Lafayette. Wife Jean. As the story goes, Gabriel moved to an Oklahoma Indian reservation, and I know of only one instance when my father and a couple of his sisters visited. I had heard about visits by Gabriel to Lafayette before 1956, but have no direct knowledge. I have attempted to get Jean's family name, but I ran into a brick wall.
5. Ida, born January 13, 1899 in Lafayette. Married Carl Robinson.
6. Jules Oscar, Monsignor Jules Daigle, born December 4, 1900 in Lafayette.
7. Anna (Anne), born March 6, 1902 in Lafayette. Married Edgar Sowar.
8. Marie Lucille, born February 8, 1904 in Lafayette. Married Joseph LaPorte.
9. Joseph Armond, born March 12, 1906 in Lafayette. (Brother Basil Gabriel Daigle)
10. Hilda (Sister Teresita)
11. George Andre, born July 25, 1909 in Lafayette. Married Henrietta Senac
12. Theresa (Sister Berchmans)
13. Mildred, married Martin Monies.

14.Lydia, married Paul Schoeffler.
15.Rose, married Larry Falcon.
16.Florence, married Felix Boudreaux.
17.Lloyd, married Doris Westbury.

From Lafayette Parish Historical Records, St. John Catholic Parish:
Francois Daigle b: April 26, 1826 Opelousas, LA d: April 04, 1874 Lafayette, LA (*Great Grandpa*) + Leocade Boudreau b: February 1833 Lafayette, LA m: June 27, 1850 Lafayette, LA (*Great Grandma*)
Gabriel Oscar Daigle b: September 02, 1869 Lafayette, LA d: January 1946 LA (*Grandpa*) + Gertrude Boudreaux b: October 04, 1869 Lafayette, LA m: June 15, 1887 Lafayette, LA d: October 28, 1887 Lafayette, LA
*2nd Wife of Gabriel Oscar Daigle: + Eliza Landry (*Grandma*) b: April 19, 1876 m: January 25, 1893 Lafayette, LA d: August 1958 LA
Regina, born October 14, 1893 in Lafayette
Edward Oscar, born December 27, 1894

Generation 11

Edward Oscar Daigle, Sr. was born December 27, 1894 in Lafayette, La. and died March 29, 1986 in Garyville, La. He married Leah Schexnayder on September 20, 1920 in Welcome, La., St. James Parish. Leah Schexnayder was born January 6, 1902 in St. Phillip, La. and she died October 26, 1962 in Garyville. (Lutcher Hospital)
Children:
Vernon Edward Married Helen Kruger
Children: Michael Vernon, John Edward, Robert

Joseph, Dianne, Theresa, Janice Marie, Catherine Elaine, William Bryan.

Lloyd Charles, born March 16, 1926. Married Marian Anne Triche December 18, 1948 Children: Lloyd Charles, Joseph Curtis, Thomas John, Neal James, Marian Anne, Lynn Charles.

Claribel Marie, born September 27, 1934. Married January 19, 1952 in Paulina by a Justice of the Peace. The official church marriage to Francis Luminais was June 5, 1952 in Garyville. Children: Eric Francis, born September 22, 1975. [Claribel and Carl were twins]

Carl Joseph, born September 27, 1934. Married Amelia Roussel.

Children: Carl Jr, Michelle.

Ruth Ann, born December 14, 1936

Married Clark West Giffin, Jr. December 28, 1957 Children:, Teresa Ann, Clark West III Anne Leah, David Patrick

Edward Oscar Jr., born September 27, 1944. Married Susan Ann Ayers, August 3, 1963. Children: Leslie Elizabeth, Rene Michael, Matthew Edward, Blythe Leah. [Edward was born the same date as Claribel and Carl exactly ten years later—Belle and Carl were twins]

E. O. DAIGLE SR
1895-1986

RESURRECTION PRAYER

Most merciful Father, we commend our
departed into your hands. We are filled
with the sure hope that our departed will
rise again on the Last Day with all who
have died in Christ. We thank you for
all the good things you have given
during our departed's earthly life.
O Father, in your great mercy, accept
our prayer that the Gates of Paradise
may be opened for your servant. In our
turn, may we too be comforted by the
words of faith until we greet Christ in
glory and are united with you and our
departed.
Through Christ our Lord   Amen.

MILLET FUNERAL HOME
Reserve & LaPlace, Louisiana

DAIGLE, MRS. EDWARD
Of Garyville, died at the ag
of 66 in St. James Parish Hospital
at Lutcher at 2:08 p.m. Sunday
Body at the Millet Funeral Hom
at Reserve. Services at 10 a.m
Tuesday at St. Hubert Cathol
Church, Garyville, with the Rev.
Bertis officiating. Entombment i
St. Peter Mausoleum in Reserve
Surviving are her husband; fou
sons, Vernon Daigle, Baton Roug
Lloyd C. Daigle, Reums, Carl J.
Daigle, Garyville, and Edward C
Daigle Jr., Garyville; two daugh
ters, Mrs. Francis Lombard
Garyville, and Mrs. Clark Griffin
Reserve; three sisters, Mrs. Pau
Melancon, Welcome, Mrs. C. A
Normand, Norco, and Mrs. Edga
Granoix, Donaldsonville, and thre
brothers, Walter, Michael an
Arthur Schexnayder, all of Wel
come.

"The Lord is my shepherd . . . though
through . . . the shadow of death . . .
art with me . . . THY ROD AND THY
THEY COMFORT ME . . . I will dwell
House of the Lord forever."   Bird 1

Mom & Dad– Leah Schexnayder Daigle

TO MOM AND DAD

I did not know your love until I became a parent myself. When I first touched my own children, your love for me was evident.

Through my adolescence and early adulthood I did not know, nor did I realize how strong your teachings would be. What profound impact your way of life would have on me. You taught without words; you taught by example.

You had your own feelings, but remained on good terms with all whom you met. You did not compare yourself with others, you accepted your role. You enjoyed your achievements and worked very hard for what you achieved. You administered a wholesome discipline, yet you could be very gentle. You surrendered to age with grace and dignity. You had great strength in times of misfortune and pain. You were always at peace with your soul and with God.

Love is the greatest thing that you gave to me and love is the greatest thing I, as your child, can give to my children and God. For if I can love God as you loved me, it will allow me to carry that love through to my children.

It is very sad that it takes death to free our feelings. Let me use this as yet another lesson from you and let me be able to share with my children, your greatest gift; love.

Edward & Leah -- Mom & Dad

Edward & Gabriel

Leah Schexnayder Daigle,
Edward Oscar Daigle, unknown

Gabriel Oscar Daigle

Belle, Lloyd, Dad

Generation 12

Edward Oscar Daigle, Jr, was born September 27, 1944 in Garyville, La. He married Susan Ann Ayers in Mandeville, La. on August 3, 1963. Susan Ann was born July 29, 1946 in New Orleans, La.

Children:

Leslie Elizabeth, born February 9, 1964. Married Arthur Price on December 14, 1984.

Rene Michael, born January 4, 1965. Married Danielle Dufour, on April 21, 1984.

Matthew Edward, born December 26, 1969. Married Casey Stogner on April 11, 2005.

Blythe Leah, born July 20, 1976

Front Row left to right: Rene, Leslie
Back Row left to right: Blythe, Matthew

Susan Ayers Daigle & Eddie

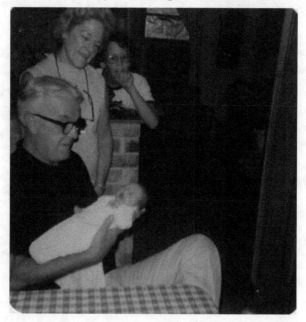

Herbie & Gammie Ayers, Rene and Baby Blythe

Edward Oscar Daigle, Sr. & Leah Schexnayder Daigle

Ruth, Helen, Belle & Leah (Mom)

The Schexnayders
(Segschneider)

The Schexnayder House, circa 1830

Typical center-hall Acadian structure. Moved from the west bank of the Mississippi River, three miles down river from the Sunshine Bridge.

The Schexnayder house is now part of the Ascension Parish Tourist stop at Highway 70 and Highway 22 in Sorrento.

92% of all Schexnayders (der) in the U.S. live in Louisiana.

Typical Slave House for Two Families

There are still many of these houses between Taft and Donaldsonville

Josef Segschneider

Die *Familien* aus

Badorf, Eckdorf, Geildorf und Pingsdorf

1625 – 1875

Deutsche Ortssippenbücher
der Zentralstelle für Personen- und Familiengeschichte
Serie A   Band 363

Westdeutsche Gesellschaft für Familienkunde e.V., Köln 2004

Used with the permission of jayschex@gmail.com

The Beginnings of the Schexnayder Family History

In St. Charles Parish, the first German Coast was the area along the river. The church serving the area was St. Charles des Allemands, St. Charles of the Germans. There were no people settled along the bayou or Lac des Allemands at the time of the the First German Coast. Those areas were settled later in the 1800s. The settlers were German farmers who contracted with John Law and his West Indies company to undertake the cultivation of farms in the lush wilderness of Louisiana. This group came from Germany, Bohemia, Switzerland, Hungary, Belgium and Austria. For the most part they were natives of Alsace, the Palatinate, and Baden.

They came in family units of parents, children, and other relatives. Having voluntarily contracted to come to Louisiana, once they departed Europe they never looked back. Even with unbelievable hardships being endured in Louisiana, they never yearned to return to their homeland.

The eighteenth-century settlers of Louisiana arrived in three groups; the first arrived between 1720 and 1738 and included the families of the Schexnayders, Edelmeiers, Zweigs, Heidels, and Himmels. Being yeoman farmers, they sought the rich farmland along the Mississippi River. They settled primarily above New Orleans in St. Charles Parish, having found deforested land which had been the site of vacated Tensas Indian villages.

The early years were a struggle with unfamiliar elements, disease, and famine, but gradually as the French joined in (Daigles arrived in 1717 or 1720), the semi-tropical jungle of St. Charles Parish was pushed back from the banks of the river and replaced by cultivated fields. Indigo was the primary crop during these times, but was replaced later in the mid-1700s as sugar cane became the primary agricultural crop.

From the records of these early years, it's apparent that the legal scribes gave up on trying to record the names of the German families in favor of simply assigning them French names – with the exception of Schexnayder, which remained on the logs and legal documents of the period in many diverse spellings that we still see today.

As a side note however, the family was not known as Schexnayder, but rather as "Albert," the name of the head of the Schexnayder clan, Albert Schexnayder. (**Segschneider**)

It is recorded that Albert and Schexnayder refer to the same family, so there is no confusion. In later years an Acadian family named Albert settled in the same area, and therefore the Schexnayders had to resume using their proper name.

Note: Schexnayder, Schexnaydre, Sexchneyder, Sexnaidre, Snydre, Sixtailleur, Seckshneyder, Secxnauder, Scheixneydre, Chisnaitre, Cheixnaydre, **Segschneider** and Hexnaider are all spellings used at some time or another in Louisiana.

The earliest of our Schexnayder ancestors is Henri Albert Schexnayder. The date of his birth is about 1709, and he died January 4, 1776. He is listed as a native of Brussels. His father was Simon Schexnayder and his mother was Anne Marie Vesdray. Since no records exist on Albert's mother and father, we assume that he came from Brussels as a child of eleven or so, and his parents did not come to this country. He was married twice; first, to Anna Maria Magdelina Wiche, and second to Marianne Edelmeir Belsom. Our direct ancestor was born of the first marriage between Henri and Marie.

Civil Records of St. Charles and St. John the Baptist Parish. Book 6 – 1776

Front Row L to R: Lou Mannina, Michel Schexnayder, Anabel Schexnayber, Anabel Torres
Back Row L to R: Millard Mannina, Joyce Schexnayder, Roland Schexnayder, Ester Schexnayder, Raymond Schexnayder, Sis Schexnayder, Edgar Schexnayder, Eva Schexnayder, Mike Schexnayder and Herman Torres

Front Row L to R: Lou Mannina, Edgar
Schexnayder, Anabel Schexnayder, Anabel Torres
    Back Row L to R: Roland Schexnayder, Raymond
Schexnayder, Edgar Schexnayder, Mike Schexnayder

Leah & Unknown

Uncle Paul Melancon & Family

LINDA   MARY LOU

LUCY SCHEXNAYDER

Schexnayders

Grandma's Birthday Party

Linda, Agnes, Mary Lou & Edgar

Agnes & Edgar

Edgar, Agnes, Mary Lou,
Linda & Richard

GRANDPA SCHEXNAYDER

Michel Francois Schexnayder

GRANDMA SCHEXNAYDER

Louise Zeringue

AGNES   AMELIA

JAMES

BOB   LEWIS   LOUIE   CARL

Grandma, Aunt Agnes,
Aunt Nee Nee

First picture of Most Rev. Maurice Schexnayder in Bishop's robes

THE MOST REVEREND
MAURICE SCHEXNAYDER

Center to Right: Leah
Daigle, Amelia Normand
and Agnes Gravois

SOME SCHEXNAYDER COUSINS
Judith Ann Sigmon
Patricia Marie Sigmon
Elizabeth Ruth Sigmon

Peggy Elaine Sigmon
Doris Ann Sigmon born May 9, 1958
Jamie Michele Petite, born June 21, 1966
Wade Paul Petite, born July 1
Brett Micheal Petite, born Feb. 26, 1971
Richard Reed Holder Jr, born Dec. 26, 1961
Robert Wayne Holder born Jan. 29, 1963
Sharon Dianne Holder born March 24, 1965
Karen Denise Holder born March 24, 1965
Edward Joseph R. Holder born May 25, 1966
Melissa Ann Holder born March 7, 1971
John Mark Ramirez Jr. born March 3, 1969
Jodi Renee Ramirez born June 17, 1971
Phyllis McCready
Walter McCready
Linda McCready born Oct. 1,
Aimie McCready born Feb. 12, 1954
Cynthia McCready
Lee Ann McCready born Oct. 29, 195?
Margaret Ann McCready born Dec. 4, 1959
Melanie Garner born Aug. 21, 1970
Waylon Garner born Dec. 3, 1973
Amber Lee Garner born June 19, 1975
Walter Joseph Schexnayder, Jr., born Sept. 30,
1921 and died Jan. 10, 1943. He was killed in
action, World War II
George Eaton Jr.
Beverly Eaton
Dennis Eaton born Nov. 28, 1954
Mary Alice Eaton born Feb. 17, 1960
George Eaton III, born June 25, 1969
Stephen Eaton born August 11, 1970
Bonnie Ann James
Deborah Ann James
Lynn Francis James born March 23, 1958

Paul Carter Prewitt born Sept. 6, 1953
Steven Charles Prewitt born Dec. 20, 1954
David Robert Prewitt born Sept. 16, 1956
Pamela Anne Prewitt born June 6, 1961
John Patrick Prewitt born Feb. 17, 1967
Renee Ann Hudspeth born Oct. 24, 1959
Lisa Ann Hudspeth born March 7, 1963
Stephen Charles Hudspeth born Oct. 24, 1964
Francis Joseph Hudspeth born Feb. 19, 1966
Carl Micheal Schexnayder born Jan. 14,1959
Catherine Ann Schexnayder born June 6, 1960
Barbara Schexnayder born Sept. 17, 1964
Melissa Ann Schexnayder born Sept. 29, 1966
Lizabeth Anne Schexnayder born August 16, 1971
Michel Francis Schexnayder I
Russel James Schexnayder
Gail Lucy Schexnayder born Dec. 6, 1953
Carl Joseph Schexnayder born Jan. 13, 1957
Jean Marie Schexnayder born January , 1974
Paul Landry Schexnayder born October, 1975
Annabel C. Newitt
Shirley Louise Hewitt
Karen A. Torres
Lloyd J. Torres born 1941 - Died at birth
Herman Francis Torres Jr. born September 2, 1950
Donna Wood born March 12, 1959
Janel Wood born July 22, 1960
Mary Lynn Wood born January 28, 1965
Lisa A. Usey born May 5, 1962
Twins-David born March 28, 1963
Darryl Usey
Carla A. Hidal born September 18, 1968
Edgar Joseph Schexnayder Jr.
Nary Susan Schexnayder
Gary James Schexnayder

Robin Schexnayder born April 21, 195?
Leah Denise Schexnayder born December 3, 1966
Julie Marie Schexnayder born January 5, 1968
Sheri Lynne Schexnayder born February 15, 1971
Edgar Joseph Schexnayder born January 10, 1975
Bentley Chris Folse born September 1, 1974
Gary James Schexnayder Jr. born September 29, 1972
Angela Lynne Schexnayder born March 2, 1975
Jason Paul Schexnayder born July 23, 1976
Leslie Marie Mannina
Joan Ann Manniatt born August 17, 1953
Micheàl Stephen Mannina
David Paul Mannina born October 23, 1955
John Millard Mannina born April 21, 195?
Mary Louise Mannina born September 27, 1959
Richard James Mannina born February 1, 1961
Carrie Lorraine Mannina born June 17, 1962
Robert Patrick I born September 29, 1961
Brian Loui Fat'cheaux born November 23, 1971
Erica Ann Mannina born July 22, 1976
Deborah Ann Schexnayder born October 10, 1955
Craig Joseph Schexnayder born June 27, 1959
Raymond Stephan Schexnayder born January 21, 1959
Sara Lynn Schexnayder born July 2 1960
Donald Mark Schexnayder born August 24, 1961
Randall Bryan Schexnayder born September 28, 1962
Dani James Schexnayder born J 17, 1964
Wanda Anne Schexnayder born December 30, 1967
Brice Timothy Schexnayder born December 23, 1970
Katherine Lucy Schexnayder
Kenneth Louie Schexnayder born April 24, 1958

Karen Marie Schexnayder born February 2, 1960
Tracy Elizabeth Schexnayder born April 25, 1962
Brent Joseph Schexnayder born September 2, 1966
Robert Paul Schexnayder born February 9, 1962
David Charles Schexnayder born August 12, 1963
Lucy Ann Schexnayder born July 18, 1964
Dale Edward Schexnayder born November 6, 1965
Neal Joseph Schexayder born January 12, 1967
Connie Ann Schexnayder born April 20, 1964
Susan Ann Schexnayder born January 24, 1967
Brian Paul Schexnayder born July 29, 1963
Barry Thomas Schexnayder born July 13, 1964
Brenda Ann Schexnayder born January 5, 1966
Jan Louise Schexnayder born February 9, 1967
Mary Ann Schexnayder born June 2, 1964 - died
June in 1964
Dennis Jude Schexnayder born July 14, 1965
Chris Jerome Schexnayder born July 2, 1966
Glenn Philip Schexnayder born May 13, 196
Dana Michelle Schexnayder born October 17, 1972
Paul Anthony Gautreau born November 5, 1971
Randy Joseph Gautreau born November 15, 1972
Micheal Melancon born February 21, 1951 died
Feb. 22, 1951
David Melancon born December 29, 1953 died
October 21, 1954
Jeanne Melancon born July 8, 1955
Denise Melancon born October 23, 1956
Stephan Melancon born May 10, 1960
Charlotte Melancon born October 20, 1961
Leonard Joseph Smith
Susan Marie Smith born December 3, 1957
Judy Eileen Smith born September 13, 1962
Stacie Ann Melancon born July 23, 1960
Dana Elizabeth Melancon born December 13, 1961

Paul Stanislaus Melancon III born August 7, 1964
Amy Marie Melancon born May 12, 196?
Michael Paul Charlet born July 12, 1960
Robert Lynn Charlet born December 19, 1962
Timothy James Charlet born January 10, 1964
Renee Ann Charlet born September ??(iS), 1966
Thomas Edward Labat Jr. born April 20, 1959
Jacinta Cecile Labat born June 6, 1960 - died
September 25, 1967
Ann Marie Labat born September 9, 1962
Nancy Anne Schexnayder born February 21, 1966
Beverly Yiarie Schexnayder born January 27, 1967
Arthur John Schexnayder born January 26, 196?
Mary Alice Schexnayder born October 10, 1970
Nark Edward Schexnayder born October 31, 1961
Patrick Joseph Schexnayder born February 23,
1963
Amy Marie Schexnayder born September 14, 19??
Stephen Schexnayder born November 16, 1965
Virginia Nary born March 27, 1967
Nathan Keith Schexnayder born December 17,
1970
Alicia Eileen Schexnayder born March 12, 1973
Jessi Lane Schexnayder born July 2 1975

Mom's Brothers and Sisters

Walter   Michael   Lionel   Arthur

Leonie   Agnes   Grandma (Louisa)   Leah

Arthur – died 11-15-73

Mike   3-19-91

Lionel   6-8-59

Walter   3-12-91

Louisa   1-6-60

Leonie

Agnes   7-5-92

Aunt Mae Cornelia

Walter Joseph Schexnayder (uncle), born in St. Phillip, St. James Parish, on October 8, 1893, married Aimee Schexnayder, born September 4,1895, in St. Phillip. They were married on Jan. 24,1917 in St. Phillip Catholic Church. Walter Schexnayder died Feb. 6,1963. To this union the following children were born:

Doris Therese

Vivian

Walter Joseph Jr.
Alice Rita
Enola Marie
Gloria
Irving James
Lorraine Cecile

Michel Francois Schexnayder (uncle), born in St. Philip, St. James Parish, April 19, 1895. On June 11, 1917 married Anabel Bertaut of St. James Parish, born October 10, 1897 and died June 1, 1970. To this union were born the following:
Michel Francis Jr.
Anabel Beatrice
Edgar Joseph
Marie Louisa
Roland Joseph
Raymond Steven

Lionel Louis Schexnayder (uncle), born October 27, 1896, married Beatrice Labiche, born Feb. 4, 1906. Lionel died June 8, 1959 and Beatrice died September 17, 1988. To this union were born the following:
Lucy Ann (born October 14, 1929, died Feb. 6, 1947)
Louis Lionel
Robert Joseph
James Adam
Sidney Joseph
Henry Paul
George Paul
Joan Ann

Leonie Marie Schexnayder (aunt), born August 20, 1898 in St. Philip, St. James Parish and died October 3, 1979. Married January 24, 1924 in St. James Catholic Church to Paul Stanislaus Melancon, born May 30, 1901 in Napoleonville, La. and died September 29, 1990. To this union were born the following:

Allen Joseph
Mildred Mary
Paul S. Jr. (Stanislaus)
Dorothy Cecile

Front Row L to R: Aunt Nee Nee, Uncle Mike, Back Row L to R: Uncle Paul, Aunt Agnes, Uncle Edgar, Aunt Amelia, Edward Daigle

Fran, Aunt Amelia, Jeanne
George, Ethel, Louie

Amelia Schexnayder (aunt), born March 17, 1907 St. Philip, St. James Parish and died August 8, 1991. November 2, 1934 married Clifton Normand, born November 10, 1909. To this union was born one child:

Louis Joseph Normand, Born August 7, 1936 died August 1, 2014.

Arthur John Schexnayder (uncle), born Oct. 16, 1908 in St. Phillip, St. James Parish, died Nov. 15, 1973. Married Alice Mary Ann Chauvin on Nov. 6, 1935 at St. Mary's Chapel, Union, La. Alice was born Feb. 11, 1911 in Union, La. and died on

August 17, 1969. To this union were born the following:
Alice Mary Ann
Arthur John Jr.
Eugene Joseph
Lawrence Anthony
Brenda Chauvin, foster daughter

Agnes Marie Schexnayder (aunt), born on Jan. 23, 1911 in St. Phillip, St. James Parish, died July 5, 1992. Married on August 23, 1941 to Edgar Gravôis, born April 16, 1914 in St. James Parish died July 8, 1993 . To this union were born the following:
Mary Lou Gravois, born March 23, 1947, married Dobbins A. Guillot
Linda Gravois, born May 26, 1948, married Richard Johnson

Leah Antonia Schexnayder (Mom)
Leah Schexnayder, born January 6, 1902, in St. Philip, St. James Parish, was married on September 20, 1920 to Edward O. Daigle, Sr., born December 27, 1894. Leah Schexnayder died October 28, 1962. The children of Leah Schexnayder and Edward Daigle, Sr.

Vernon Edward Daigle, born December 12, 1923, married Helen Krueger Daigle who was born on January 23, 1926. Children born of this union are:
Michael Vernon Daigle, Born October 13, 1945
John Edward Daigle, Born August 2, 1948
Robert Joseph Daigle, Born May 28, 1951

Diane Theresa Daigle, Born February 19, 1958

Janice Marie Daigle, Born October 20, 1959

Catherine Elaine Daigle, Born July 7, 1962

William Brian Daigle, Born November 14, 1963

Lloyd Charles Daigle, married Marion Triche. Lloyd Daigle died July 20, 1974. Children born of this union are:

Lloyd C. Daigle---Born October 11, 1949

Joseph C. Daigle---Born December 4, 1950

Thomas J. Daigle---Born December 14, 1951

Neil J. Daigle---Born March 7, 1954

Lynn Daigle---Born March 13, 1960

Marian---Born November 20, 1961

Claribel Marie Daigle, born September 27, 1934, married Francis Keller Luminais, who was born September 8, 1932. The child born of this marriage is:

Eric Francis Luminais – Born September 22, 1975

Carl Joseph Daigle, born September 27, 1934, married Amelia Roussel, born December 26, 1941, and to this marriage was born the following children.

Carl J. Daigle, Jr – Born November 7, 1964

Michelle Daigle – Born August 31, 1967

Amelia & Carl Sr.

Ruth Ann Daigle, born December 14, 1936, married Clark V. Giffin Jr., who was born on August 8, 1936. The marriage took place on December 28, 1957. Children born of this union are:

Theresa Ann Giffin – Born January 31, 1959
Clark W. Giffin III – Born July 19, 1961
Anne Leah Giffin – Born November 2, 1965
David Patrick Giffin – Born July 2, 1970

Edward Oscar Daigle, Jr., born September 27, 1944, married Susan Ayers, born July 29, 1946. Marriage was August 3, 1963 Children born of this union are:

Leslie Elizabeth Daigle – Born February 9, 1964
René Michael Daigle – Born January 4, 1965
Matthew Edward Daigle – Born December 26, 1969.
Bythe Leah Daigle – Born July 20, 1976

Carl, Rex & Eddie

Belle, Susan & Amelia

Schexnayder Genealogy

Generation 1

Simon Schexnayder – Born 1694 possibly in Brussels, Belgium. (no proof of this) Married to Anne Marie Vesdray of Brussels, born 1690 and married 1705.

Name Spelling: Segschneider
Children:

Henri Albert Schexnayder – arrived in Louisiana 1721. Married to Anna Maria Magdalena Wiche, born in Stebbach, Germany (no other children are listed). There is also confusion between Anna Maria Magdalena Huisine some has listed at the wife. Note the two names.

Note: Birth dates, marriage dates in generation one leads to some confusion as to the actual date Henri Albert arrived in Louisiana and how old he was when he arrived. In many legal documents from St. Charles Parish, Henri Albert Schexnayder was simply listed as "Albert" due to the difficult spelling of Schexnayder or one of its many other forms.

Name	Albert Scheckschneider (Segschneider)
Arrival Year	1721
Arrival Place	Louisiana
Family Members	With wife; Son Scheckschneider, Albert
Source Publication Code	1497.15
Primary Immigrant	Scheckschneider, Hans Reinhard
Annotation	Date and port of arrival, date and place of census, or date and place of mention in the New World. Exhaustive historical and genealogical information is also provided.
Source Bibliography	DEILER, J. HANNO. The Settlement of the German Coast of Louisiana and the Creoles of German Descent. Baltimore, MD: Clearfield Co., Inc., 1998. 154p.

Generation 2

Henri Albert Schexnayder – Born in Brussels 1709, Belgium. Arrived in Louisiana in 1721. Died January 4, 1776 in St. Charles Parish, Louisiana. Married to Anna Maria Magdelina Wiche, born in Belgium, died in the vicinity of Taft. This marriage produced ten children:

Henri Albert
George
Ambrose
Margarita

Catherine
Josette
Julianne
Jean Baptist
Adam
Andre
The second marriage to Marianne Edelmier produced one child:
Epiphany

Generation 3

Andre Schexnayder – Born in St. Charles Parish 1729. Married Marie Catherine Rixner. The marriage produced eight children.
Joseph
Andre Jr.
Jean Lebert
George Jean
Toussaint
Marguerite
Magdelaine
Marie Josephe

Generation 4

Andre Albert Schexnayder – Born 1767 in Taft, La. Died November 1, 1832 in Taft, La. Married to Rosalie Haydel, born 1767 in Taft, La., daughter of Jean George Haydel and Marie Leroux.
Children:
Henri Schexnayder, born 1796 and died February 28, 1861. Married Marianne Champagne, born 1797, on May 19, 1818, the daughter of Jean Baptist Champagne and Catherine Waguespack.

Euphrosine
Clemence
Caliste
Marcellite
Adeline
Constance
Celeste
Albert Joseph
Rosalie
Florestine
Anastasia
Melasie

Generation 5

Henri Schexnayder – Born 1796 in Taft, died February 28, 1861. Married Marianne Champagne, born 1797, on May 19, 1818. The daughter of Jean Baptist Champagne and Catherine Waguespack.
Children:
Andre
Valsin

Adam Lucien Schexnayder, born December 17, 1834. On May 12, 1855 he married Marie Agnes Tregre, born July 16, 1839, daughter of Onesime Tregre & Francoise Dufresne.
Eve Florestine.
Damose Emile
Marianne Irma
Florestan Henry
Pamela Catherine
Theodule Jean Baptiste
Evariste

Generation 6

Adam Schexnayder – born December 17, 1834. On May 12, 1855 he married Marie Agnes Tregre, born July 16, 1839, daughter of Onesime Tregre and Francoise Dufrense.
Children:
Francois Michel Schexnayder – Born October 6, 1862 Wallace. Died December 1, 1928 in St. Philip, Vacherie, Louisiana. Married Louisa Zeringue.
Joseph
Adam Jr.
Alisia Eve
Henry Joseph
Marie Anne Francoise
Agnes Marie

Generation 7

Francois Michel Schexnayder – born October 6, 1862, Wallace, La. died December 1, 1928. In 1892, in St. Phillip Catholic Church in Vacherie, he married Marie Louisa Zeringue, born September 8, 1874, died June 6, 1960. Daughter of Louis Zeringue and Eveline Marie Moncondiut.
Children:
Walter Joseph, born October 18, 1893. Married Aimee Schexnayder January 24, 1917.
Michel Francis, born April 19, 1895. Married Anabel Bertaut, June 11, 1917.
Lionel Louis, born October 27, 1897. Married Beatrice LaBiche, November 7, 1928.

Leonie Marie, born August 20, 1899. Married Paul Melancon January 23, 1924.

Leah, born January 6, 1902. Married Edward Daigle, September 20, 1920.

** Adelta (died as a small child)

Amelia, born March 17, 1907. Married Cilton Normand November 28, 1934.

Arthur, born October 16, 1908. Married Alice Mary Ann Chauvin Nov. 6, 1935.

Agnes, born January 23, 1911. Married Edgar Gravois August 23, 1941.

** Adelta Marie born February 10, 1904, Baptized at St. Philip February 13, 1904. Died April 8, 1904 buried at St. Philip April 9, 1904.

Generation 8

Leah Schexnayder – born January 6, 1902, in St. Phillip, and married September 20, 1920 to Edward O. Daigle, Sr. born December 27, 1894. Leah died October 28, 1962. Edward died March 29, 1986.

Children:

Vernon, born December 12, 1923 Married Helen Kruger.

Lloyd, born died 1974 Married Marion Triche.

Claribel, born September 27, 1934 Married Francis Luminais.

Carl, born September 27, 1934 Married Amelia Roussel.

Ruth Ann, born December 14, 1936. Married Clark W. Giffin December 28, 1957.

Edward O. Daigle, Jr., born September 27, 1944. Married Susan Ann Ayers, August 3, 1963.

Back Row L to R: Marian, Claribel, Carl, Ruth Ann, Helen
Middle Row L to R: Lloyd, Edward Sr, Leah, Vernon
Front Row L to R: Mike, Edward Jr.

Generation 9

Edward O. Daigle, Jr. - born September 27, 1944. Married to Susan Ann Ayers of New Orleans, born July 29, 1946, on August 3, 1963 in Mandeville, La.

Children:
Leslie Elizabeth, born February 9, 1964.
Rene Michael, born January 4, 1965.
Matthew Edward, born December 26, 1969.
Blythe Leah, born July 20, 1976.

Matthew, Rene, Blythe & Leslie Daigle

Notable Schexnayders From the Many Louisiana Families

Dr. Clifford Schexnayder - Eminent Scholar Emeritus at the Del E. Webb School of Construction at Arizona State University. He is described as the world's leading authority on construction equipment and has authored the most widely used text in the field, worldwide.

Bishop Maurice Schexnayder - installed in 1956, he headed the Diocese of Lafayette. He is a native of Wallace (Vacherie) Louisiana and was ordained in 1925 in the Archdiocese of New Orleans. A former chaplain of the LSU Catholic Student Center, he came to Lafayette from St. Francis de Sales Parish, Houma, where he was pastor. He attended the Second Vatican Council and issued pastoral letters implementing its decrees. Bishop Schexnayder was an early advocate of lay participation and issued many pastoral letters which warned against neglect or interference in this area.

Irving "Boo" Schexnayder - considered one of the nation's premier field events coaches. Boo serves as Chair of the Jumps program of USA Track and Field Coaching Education, and is also the national chair of USA Education and Biomechanics, Track and Field. He has numerous training manuals, books, and electronic media for Track and Field competition and training regimes. Boo was the Director of CAP Elite Training Center for the 2008 USA US Olympics. He is a USATF Master Coach.

Nelson Schexnayder - recently resigned as Athletic Director of ULL after 12 years in the post. He will remain at the University in another position. Schexnayder led a Ragin' Cajun athletic program that passed many milestones, including NCAA men's basketball tournament appearances, a best-ever season for the women's basketball team, a trip to the College World Series in baseball, and the building of a national reputation by the softball team.

Donnie Schexnayder - is a ministry technology expert. He has 10 years of experience in supporting churches and Christian ministries with technology. He helps them bring the gospel of Jesus Christ to the ends of the earth by using cutting edge recording technology.

Richard Schexnayder - has won an Emmy in 1994 for Outstanding Sound Mixing for a Drama Series, The Stand. He has been nominated for Emmys on three other occasions; 1989 Margaret Bourke-White (TV), 1995 CAS Award for The Stand, and 2005 for Faith of My Fathers. Some of the programs he has worked on include Racing for Time; The Staircase Murders; Heartless; Local Color; Boy Meets Boy; The Agency; Impostor; Gilmore Girls; the Magnificent Seven; The Shining; Lois & Clark; The New Adventures of Superman; Tales from the Crypt, and many others.

Albert J. Schexnayder - Award winning artist. He is well known throughout the US for his work in watercolor, but he also produces etchings and works with pen and ink, pencil, egg tempera, and acrylic. His works have been selected for several North American tours by the American

Watercolor Society, Watercolor USA, and Watercolor Art Society International. His paintings and limited edition prints are included in many private and corporate collections throughout the US and abroad.

Paul Schexnayder - Never having formal art lessons or even holding a paintbrush until he reached college, Paul graduated from LSU with a degree in Fine Arts. After graduation he taught at the Boston Landmark School for students with learning differences, and through extensive travels in Guatemala and Mexico, he began to define his own personal style as narrative. The Boston Globe described his paintings as "an exciting patchwork of color." His roots in South Louisiana called him home in the early 1990s, and he returned to make his home in New Iberia. His paintings have been described as having a rhythm and charged movement that creates both an emotional and physical stir. Paul has shown in numerous group, juried and solo shows throughout the U.S. and abroad, and his paintings hang in many private collections. Visit www.schex.com

Steve Schexnayder - Pediatric Care Specialist. Named the first recipient of the Betty Ann Lowe Distinguished Chair in Pediatric Education.

Michael Schexnayder - Deputy Commander for Research, Development and Acquisition at the US Army Space and Missile Defense Command, Strategic Command, Redstone Arsenal. He oversees test and evaluation activities for Space and Missile Defense Future Warfare and the High Energy Laser System located at White Sands, NM. A graduate of LSU, a Master of

Science from Georgia Institute of Technology, and an MS in management as a Sloan Fellow from the Massachusetts Institute of Technology. As an Army officer he was an Airborne Ranger.

Mark Schexnayder - Known as "Watermarks," Mark serves as a regional coastal advisor for fisheries in the Louisiana Sea Grant College program at LSU. He is the past Director of the Marine Biological Lab on Grand Terre and manager of the state crustacean program. Mark is spearheading a local and national program to save Louisiana's coastal marshes.

CONFUSION

Using the map above of the original counties (parishes later) you again see why so much confusion reigns when tracing ancestry and dates. Note that the "Acadia" county is in Southeast Louisiana next to the German Coast. Many records become confused, especially when tracking the French-Canadian Daigles (our family) and the Acadians expelled from Canada many years later in the Grand Derangement.

DIVERGENCE and CONVERGENCE:
The Brothers Daigle, Olivier Daigle, and the Schexnayders

THE BROTHERS

It is documented that Etienne left two brothers in Canada when he left for Louisiana between 1711 and 1720. These brothers, Chevalier and Alexandre, are said to have followed him some years later, and records indicate that they went straight to Plaquemine Brulée upon arriving in Louisiana. That creates the logical assumption of why Etienne left St. Charles Parish and made his home in the town that would become Church Point. However, according to the genealogy of Monsignor Jules, no brothers with those names are listed.

There are other documents indicating that two brothers ended up in Louisiana as exiles during the Grand Derangement and that they were siblings of Etienne's, but this is doubtful given that this horrific event happened in 1755, and it was Acadians who were exiled, not Quebecois French Canadians. Had the brothers been Etienne's, they would have been elderly both for the times and the journey, even if they had arrived in the very first year of the exile – which is doubtful, since it took the Acadians quite some years to find their way to Louisiana. Of course, almost anything is possible, and we've seen that after his death, two of Jean's sons were in the Daigle home at Bourg-Royal until its sale in 1708, but there is no record of Etienne's brothers moving from Quebec to Acadia that I've found.

It's interesting to note, however, that Etienne III had a son, Joseph Chevalier, from whom we are descended.

Many want to think of our family as Acadians. Yes, we are Cajuns culturally, historically indistinguishable in language, custom, and religion, but we are not Acadians. While there is some confusion in the records as to when our family actually came to Louisiana, there is none regarding our French Canadian ancestry and our arrival before the Grand Derangement. While our direct ancestor Jean was not an Acadian exiled in 1755 from Nova Scotia, it is known that Daigles who had remained in the province were among the Acadians sent to Louisiana. There were no doubt some in our direct lineage such as Leocade Boudreaux, Charles Landry, Ida Chaisson, who all trace back to Acadie.

OLIVIER DAIGLE

There are documents that strongly suggest that the Acadian Daigles – mostly those dispersed throughout southeastern Louisiana – are descended from Olivier Daigle. Some researchers believe there was a family relationship between the French Canadian Jean D'Aigle and the Acadian Olivier Daigle, while others do not. It's likely that there was a familial relation at some time and they are reasonable assumptions, but with the records found so far, knowing exactly when has generated disagreement among researchers.

Olivier's descendants lived in the Port Royal and Grand Pré areas of Nova Scotia. In 1755, some of them were deported to Virginia, which refused to take any Acadians. One group was then sent to England as prisoners of war for seven years before being released to France, where many lived for decades. Another group ended up in Louisiana as part of the expelled Acadians.

Regarding the group sent to France, the government of Spain needed people to come to Louisiana, which it owned. So in an agreement with France, the Olivier family and others were sent to Louisiana. They settled in Bayou Lafourche, Houma, and some in the area around St. Gabriel and Baton Rouge. They are possibly all descended from the same family.

Many ships carrying Daigles sailed from France to New Orleans. Of eleven Daigle families recorded as arriving in 1785, one remained in New Orleans while seven established homes along the Mississippi River between Manchac and Baton

Rouge. The remaining three families settled along Bayou Lafourche. Among the Manchac-Baton Rouge group was the family of one Olivier Daigle and his eight children, five sons and three daughters. It is doubtful that this is the patron of the Olivier Daigle clan; more likely it is a descendant carrying on the name. Of his children, the family of Jean-Mathurin, which included his wife Marie Levron and their four sons, migrated to the lower Teche to form another branch of the family. One son and daughter-in-law, Louis Maurice Daigle and his wife Anastasie Braud, settled in Attakapas where their descendants remain today, from Morgan City to New Iberia and the Mari's Native American area south of Jeanerette. From these eight siblings, Daigle families settled in the modern-day parishes of Lafourche, Assumption, West Baton Rouge, East Baton Rouge, Ascension, and along Bayou Lafourche through Thibodaux and down to Houma.

The Daigles in Louisiana are essentially divided into two families by ancestry and geography. The Daigles from southwest Louisiana (west of the Atchafalaya River) are generally descended from Jean Daigle, while those in southeast Louisiana are generally from the Olivier Daigle ancestry. In Southwest Louisiana the name is pronounced *Day-gul*, while in Southeast Louisiana, it is pronounced *Daig*.

Through the years many Daigles migrated back to New Orleans where they stayed, and 230 households of Daigles were listed in New Orleans before Hurricane Katrina hit.

With information from Acadian—Cajun,
Tim Hebert 1998

Note: There are two manuscripts, one a letter
written by Quorum Daigle which crosses two
families and is therefore in error in some
parts and correct in other parts. There is a
much larger unpublished manuscript
concerning the Daigle family titled *Etienne
Daigle*, written by Norwood Marcy Lyons.
This manuscript, as mentioned in his notes
quoted earlier, was carefully studied by
Uncle Jules and he pronounced Lyons' work
to be the most correct of the stories
regarding the Daigle family.

THE SCHEXNAYDERS

The Daigles came to Louisiana via French
Canada while the Schexnayders came via France.
The Daigles think of themselves as French and the
Schexnayders (**Segschneider)** think of themselves
as German. This appears confusing, but both
families originated in the area around Brussels,
Begium, and because of that country's geographic
location, approximately half of its residents speak
French and the other half speak Dutch, which is a
major Germanic language. Brussels sits in the part
of Belgium where today French is the predominant
language. There is also evidence that both families
were in Austria before moving to Brussels.

For the Schexnayder clan, as mentioned
earlier Simon Schexnayder (or **Segschneider)** was
thought to be born in Brussels in 1694, (however
there is no proof of this) and his marriage to Anne

Marie Vesdray (or Vasdray) in the early 1700s provides the earliest known history of the family. Although there is no birthdate listed for their son, Henri Albert, research indicates that he arrived in Louisiana 1721, and eventually settled in an area west of modern day Taft, St. Charles Parish, along with other pioneers, both French and German. St. Charles Parish spans both the east and west sides of the Mississippi River and was part of the pioneer community called the German Coast, (predominantly on the westbank) which hosted both French and German immigrants.

Henri was probably quite young upon his arrival, and it seems he arrived without his parents; at least there are no records of their presence that I know of. Nor is there a date for Henri Albert's first marriage, although we know that he and his wife, Anna Maria Magdelina Wiche, raised ten children. (There is confusion as to exactly who Henry married; Anne Marie Magdelina Wiche or Wich.

My DNA from 23 & Me and from Ancestry indicate similar historical origins, taking into account both my mother and father. I am 60% French and 40% German. Historically, I am 82% European (England, Scotland, Wales, France, Germany, Belgium, Austria and Italy), 8% Ireland and all other 10%. The link to both families is St. Charles Parish, in particular the community between Wallace and Taft, (thereabouts) is where both families lived and owned land. The Daigles arrived in Canada in 1674, and sometime in the years from 1717 to 1720, Etienne D'Aigle arrived in New Orleans from Charlesbourg, Quebec, was married in New Orleans to Susanne D'Esperon, and died in St. Charles Parish in the vicinity of what is now Taft. His grandson, Etienne II, died in St. Charles Parish. Henri Albert Schexnayder arrived in Louisiana between 1721 and 1738, the date is disputed. He settled in the area around Taft, the German Coast. I could not find any links beyond Simon Schexnayder who may have been born in Brussels, Belgium in 1694 and married Anne Marie Vesdray of Brussels, born 1690. Henri Albert arrived in Louisiana in 1721 and since he is mentioned in the 1732 census of German Villages as "Albert" could have arrived about the same period Etienne Daigle arrived.

People and Points of Interest

Coat of Arms

In 1545, the Catholic Church made the use of a saint's name mandatory for baptism. Prior to this time, only single names were predominant with only about twenty to thirty first names used. In the early 1600s, the Protestants rejected anything associated with Catholicism and began to use names from the Old Testament.

There is a third coat of arms for Daigle, which depicts a dove holding an olive branch in its beak against a royal blue background, covered above by a soaring eagle. I did not display these arms since I could not find any direct collaborative link to them, even though the colors and the eagle are present. It may have been a later coat of arms created by a younger son.

The Daigles and Schexnayders both arrived in Louisiana about the same time, the Daigles approximately between the years 1717 and 1720, and the Schexnayders in 1721.

Sources: Societe Francaise d'Heraldique et de Sigillographie, 113 Rue de Courcelles, Paris 17, France, and Association de la Famille Daigle

SOME LOUISIANA HISTORY

French Beginnings 1698-1766

On April 9, 1682, Robert Cavelier de la Salle planted the cross on Louisiana soil and erected a plaque with the French fleur-de-lis, claiming the lower Mississippi Valley in the name of God and the French king. The Catholic colony that developed, with its center in New Orleans after 1718, quickly became one of North America's most culturally and ethnically diverse cities with residents from Europe, Africa, the Caribbean and

North American colonies such as Martinique and Canada, as well as a small number of Native Americans. The Louisiana colony formed a distant part of the Diocese of Quebec.

The first Acadians arrived in the 1760s, forty years *after* the first Daigles and Schexnayders. This is important to remember.

These are the colony's pioneer parishes and the years they were established:
Old Biloxi (Ocean Springs, Mississippi), 1699
Mobile in Alabama, 1703
Natchez in Mississippi, 1716
Robeline, 1717
New Orleans - St. Louis Church, 1720
La Balize near the mouth of the Mississippi River, 1722
The German Coast (later St. Charles in Destrehan), 1723
Point Coupee, 1728
Natchitoches, 1728
Chapitoulas (Metarie), 1729
The last seven are all in Louisiana.

In 1727, Ursuline nuns from France arrived in New Orleans to take charge of the Royal Hospital and to provide education for the colony's girls and women. They immediately began instructing African and Native American girls as well as the daughters of European settlers. Their school remains the oldest continuously operating school in the United States.

At the end of the French period, more than a half dozen permanent settlements had been established in the lower Mississippi Valley. Already,

a third generation of native-born Louisianans –
Creoles – were appearing, particularly outside of
New Orleans in lower Southeast Louisiana. Today,
many of these Creoles are referred to by the
pejorative name Sabines, a name for the mix of
African American, Caucasian (French & Spanish),
and Native American. Even today there are
communities in Southeast Louisiana whose
inhabitants are at times referred to by this name.

The Catholic Church in Louisiana

Roger Baudier

The discoverers and pioneers, De Soto,
Iberville, La Salle, Bienville, were accompanied by
missionaries in their expeditions through the
Louisiana Purchase, and in the toilsome beginnings
of the first feeble settlements, which were simply
military posts, the Cross blazed the way. From the
beginning of its history, Louisiana had been placed
under the Bishop of Quebec; in 1696 the priests of
the seminary of Quebec petitioned the second
Bishop of Quebec for authority to establish
missions in the west, investing the superior sent
out by the seminary with the powers of vicar-
general. The field for which they obtained this
authority (1 May, 1698), was on both banks of the
Mississippi and its tributaries. They proposed to
plant their first mission among the Tamarois, but
when this became known, the Jesuits claimed that
tribe as one already under their care; they received
the new missionaries with personal cordiality, but
regarded the official action of Bishop St-Vallier as
an intrusion. Fathers Jolliet de Montigny, Antoine
Davion, and François Busion de Saint-Cosme were

the missionaries sent to found the new missions in the Mississippi Valley. In 1699 Iberville, who had sailed from France, with his two brothers Bienville and Sauvolle, and Father Du Ru, S.J., coming up the estuary of the Mississippi, found Father Montigny among the Tensus Indians. Iberville left Sauvolle in command of the little fort at Biloxi, the first permanent settlement in Louisiana.

In 1703, Bishop St-Vallier proposed to erect Mobile into a parish, and to annex it in perpetuity to the seminary; the seminary agreed, and the Parish of Mobile was erected 20 July, 1703, and united to the Seminary of Foreign Missions of Paris and Quebec. Father Roulleaux de la Vente, of the Diocese of Bayeaux, was appointed parish priest and Father Huve his assistant. The Biloxi settlement being difficult to access from the sea, Bienville thought it unsuitable to be the headquarters of the province. In 1718, taking with him fifty men, he selected Tchoutchouma, the present site of New Orleans, about 110 miles from the mouth of the Mississippi, where there was a deserted Indian village. Bienville directed his men to clear the grounds and erect buildings. The city was laid out according to the plans of the Chevalier Le Blond de La Tour, chief engineer of the colony, the plans including a parish church, which Bienville decided to dedicate under the invocation of St. Louis.

The old St. Louis cathedral stands today on the site of this first parish church, and the presbytery in Cathedral Alley is the site of the first modest clergy house. Bienville called the city New

Orleans after the Duc d'Orléans, and the whole territory Louisiana, or New France.

In August, 1717, the Duc d'Orléans, as Regent of France, issued letters patent establishing a joint-stock company to be called "The Company of the West," to which Louisiana was transferred. The company was obliged to build churches at its own expense wherever it should establish settlements; also to maintain the necessary number of duly approved priests to preach, perform Divine service and administer the sacraments under the authority of the Bishop of Quebec. Bienville experienced much opposition from the Company of the West in his attempt to remove the colony from Biloxi. In 1721 Fr. Francis-Xavier de Charlevoix, S.J., one of the first historians of Louisiana, made a tour of New France from the Lakes to the Mississippi, visiting New Orleans, which he describes as "a little village of about one hundred cabins dotted here and there, a large wooden warehouse in which I said Mass, a chapel in course of construction and two storehouses".

But under Bienville's direction the city soon took shape, and, with the consent of the company, the colony was moved to this site in 1723.

Father Charlevoix reported on the great spiritual destitution of the province occasioned by the missions being scattered so far apart and the scarcity of priests, and this compelled the council of the company to make efforts to improve conditions. Accordingly, the company applied to the Bishop of Quebec, and on 16 May, 1722, Louisiana was divided into three ecclesiastical sections. The district north of the Ohio was entrusted to the Society of Jesus and the Priests of the Foreign Missions of Paris and Quebec; that between the Mississippi and the Rio Perdito, to the Discalced Carmelite Fathers with headquarters at Mobile. The Carmelites were recalled, not long after, and their district was given to the Capuchins.

A different arrangement was made for the Indian and new French settlements on the lower Mississippi. Because of the remoteness of this district from Quebec, Father Louis-François Duplessis de Mornay, a Capuchin of Meudon, was consecrated, at Bishop St-Vallier's request, coadjutor Bishop of Quebec, 22 April, 1714. Bishop St-Vallier appointed him vicar-general for Louisiana, but he never came to America, although he eventually succeeded to the See of Quebec. When the Company of the West Indies applied to him for priests for the lower Mississippi Valley he offered the more populous field of colonists to the Capuchin Fathers of the province of Champaigne, who, however, did not take any immediate steps, and it was not until 1720 that any of the order came to Louisiana. Father Jean-Matthieu de Saint-Anne is the first whose name is recorded. He signs himself in 1720 in the register of the parish of New Orleans. The last entry of the secular clergy in Mobile is that of Rev. Alexander Huve, 13 January, 1721. The Capuchins came directly from France and consequently found application to the Bishop of Quebec long and tedious; Father Matthieu therefore applied to Rome for special power for fifteen missions under his charge, representing that the great distance from the Bishop of Quebec made it practically impossible for him to apply to the Bishop. A brief was issued (Michael a Tugio, "Bullarium Ord. FF. Minor. S.P. Francisci Capucinorum", Fol. 1740-52; BLI., pp. 322, 323), and Father Matthieu seems to have assumed that it exempted him from episcopal jurisdiction, for, on 14 March, 1723, he signs the register "Père Matthieu, Vicaire Apostolique et Curé de la Mobile".

In 1722 Bishop Mornay entrusted the spiritual jurisdiction of the Indians to the Jesuits, who were to establish missions in all parts of Louisiana with residence at New Orleans, but were not to exercise any ecclesiastical function there without the consent of the Capuchins, though they were to minister to the French in the Illinois District, with the Priests of the Foreign Missions, where the superior of each body was a vicar-general, just as the Capuchin superior was at New Orleans. In the spring of 1723 Father Raphael du Luxembourg arrived to assume his duties as superior of the Capuchin Mission in Louisiana. It was a difficult task that the Capuchins had assumed. Their congregations were scattered over a large area; there was much poverty, suffering, and ignorance of religion.

Father Raphael, in the cathedral archives, says that when he landed in New Orleans he could hardly secure a room for himself and his brethren to occupy pending the rebuilding of the presbytery, much less one to convert into a chapel; for the population seemed indifferent to all that savored of religion. There were less than thirty persons at Mass on Sundays; yet, undismayed, the missionaries set to work and saw their zeal rewarded with a greater reverence for religion and more faithful attendance at church. In 1725 New Orleans had become an important settlement, the Capuchins having a flock of six hundred families. Mobile had declined to sixty families, the Apache Indians (Catholic) numbered sixty families. There were six at Balize, two hundred at St. Charles or Les Allemandes, one hundred at Point Coupée, six at Natchez, fifty at Natchitoches and the other missions which are not named in the "Bullarium Capucinorum" (Vol. VIII, p. 330).

Meanwhile, Father Mathurin le Petit, S.J. established a mission among the Chocktaws; Father Du Poisson among the Arkansas; Father Doutreleau, on the Wabash; Fathers Tartarin and Le Boulenger, at Kaskaskia; Father Guymonneau among the Metchogameas; Father Souel, among the Yazoos; Father Baudouin, among the Chickasaws. The Natchez Indians, provoked by the tyranny and rapacity of Chopart, the French commandant, in 1729 nearly destroyed all these missions. Father Du Poisson and Father Souel were killed by the Indians. As an instance of the faith implanted in the Iroquois about this time there was received into the Ursuline order at New Orleans, Mary Turpin, daughter of a Canadian Father and an Illinois mother. She died a professed nun in 1761, at the age of fifty-two, with the distinction of being the first American-born nun in this country. From the beginning of the colony at Biloxi the immigration of women had been small. Bienville made constant appeals to the mother country to send honest wives and mothers. From time to time ships freighted with girls would arrive. They came over in charge of the Grey Nuns of Canada and a priest, and were sent by the king to be married to the colonists. The Bishop of Quebec was also charged with the duty of sending out young women who were known to be good and virtuous. As a proof of her respectability, each girl was furnished by the bishop with a curiously wrought casket. They are known in Louisiana history as "casket girls". Each band of girls, on arriving at New Orleans, was confided to the care of the Ursulines until they were married to colonists able to provide for their support. Many of the best families of the state are proud to trace their descent from "casket girls."

The city was growing and developing. A better class of immigrant was pouring in, and Father Charlevoix, on his visit in 1728, wrote to the Duchesse de Lesdiguières: "My hopes, I think, are well-founded that this wild and desert place, which the reeds and trees still cover, will be one day, and that not far distant, a city of opulence, and the metropolis of a rich colony." His words were prophetic. New Orleans was fast developing, and early chronicles say that it suggested the splendors of Paris. There was a governor with a military staff, bringing to the city the manners and splendors of the Court of Versailles, and the manners and usages of the mother country stamped on Louisiana life characteristics in marked contrast to the life of any other colony. The Jesuit Fathers of New Orleans had no parochial residence, but directed the Ursulines, and had charge of their private chapel and a plantation where, in 1751, they introduced into Louisiana the culture of the sugarcane, the orange, and the fig. The Capuchins established missions wherever they could. Bishop St-Vallier had been succeeded by Bishop de

Mournay, who never went to Quebec, but resigned the See, after five years.

His successor, Henri-Marie Du Breuil de Pontbriand, appointed Father de Beaubois, S.J., his vicar-general in Louisiana. The Capuchin Fathers refused to recognize Father de Beaubois's authority, claiming, under an agreement of the Company of the West with the coadjutor bishop, de Mornay, that the superior of the Capuchins was, in perpetuity, vicar-general of the province, and that the bishop could appoint no other.

Succeeding bishops of Quebec declared, however, that they could not, as bishops, admit that the assent of a coadjutor and vicar-general to an agreement with a trading company had forever deprived every bishop of Quebec to act as freely in Louisiana as in any other part of his diocese. This incident gave rise to some friction between the two orders which has been spoken of derisively by Louisiana historians, notably by Gayarré, as "The War of the Capuchins and the Jesuits." Father Boudoin, S.J., the benefactor of the colony, who had introduced the culture of sugarcane and oranges from San Domingo, and figs from Provence, a man to whom the people owed much and to whom Louisiana today owes so much of its prosperity, alone remained. He was now seventy-two years old and had spent thirty-five years in the colony. He was broken in health and too ill to leave his room. They dragged him through the streets when prominent citizens intervened and one wealthy planter, Etienne de Boré, who had first succeeded in the granulation of sugar, defied the authorities and took Father Boudoin to his home and sheltered him until his death in 1766. The most monstrous part of the order of expulsion was that, not only were the chapels of the Jesuits in lower Louisiana – many of which were the only places where Catholics, whites and Indians, and negroes, could worship God – leveled to the ground, but the Council carried out the decree even in the Illinois district which had been ceded to the King of England and which was no longer subject to France or Louisiana. They ordered even the vestments and plate to be delivered to the king's attorney. Thus was a vast territory left destitute of priests and altars, and the growth of the Church retarded for many years. Of the ten Capuchins left to administer this immense territory, five were retained in New Orleans; the remainder were scattered over various missions. It is interesting to note that the only native Louisiana priest at this time, and the first to enter the holy priesthood, Rev. Bernard Viel, born in New Orleans 1 October, 1736, was among the Jesuits expelled from the colony. He died in France, 1821. The inhabitants of New Orleans then numbered four thousand.

The Catholic Church and Slavery in Early South Louisiana

Excerpts from *New Orleans As It Was* by Henry C. Castellanos

The practice of Catholicism extended across racial boundaries in colonial Louisiana, and interracial worship continued to characterize the religious experience of Catholics throughout the antebellum period. French and Spanish missionaries baptized natives, settlers, and slaves, and the Catholic Church required Catholic planters to baptize and catechize their slaves.

Enslaved persons in the river parishes of Louisiana integrated Catholic rituals into their expressions of spirituality. Slaves' uses of herbs, medicinal practices, Voodoo, ghost-lore, and folk stories combined their experiences as enslaved persons and their contact with Catholic teachings to inform themselves of worldviews and the Catholic-Christianity of all parishioners in southeast Louisiana.

Catholic veneration of saints and prayers for the dead also fit into slaves' conceptions of spirituality. At a basic level, practitioners of Voodoo and Catholicism shared the belief that the spiritual world could influence and change physical reality, an attractive tenet for enslaved persons, who had few, if any, opportunities to change the world they lived in. Indeed, nineteenth-century New Orleanians observed the attraction of Voodoo for both white and black Catholics because of its promise to shape aspects of reality – love, health, death – through spirituality. In New Orleans, Marie Laveau and her daughter popularized the practice of Voodoo.

Central to Voodoo and hoodoo was a priest, priestess, or other figure who served as a human link between the spiritual and the physical. Father Paret, of course, could hardly have claimed such a role, but he certainly enabled the double connection evident to river parish slave spirituality - slaves' personal beliefs linked to Catholic religious tradition, physical linked to spiritual reality. At the least, priests like Paret complicate descriptions of the "priest" or "medicine-man" of plantations.

Excerpt from *No Cross, No Crown: Black Nuns in Nineteenth-Century New Orleans* by Sister Mary Bernard Diggs

For free women of color, the Catholic Church offered particular opportunities to extend their religious, social, and economic standings. In the river parishes outside New Orleans, free women of color demonstrated their piety and their financial resources by engaging in economic exchanges with local churches. In New Orleans proper, a group of free women of color formed the Sisters of the Holy Family, the first order solely for women of African-American descent, in order to aid ill and needy blacks.

The Catholic Church had neither huge successes nor absolute failure among African-American parishioners during the eighteenth and nineteenth centuries. The experiences of free women of color in South Louisiana proved that some blacks found religious, as well as social and economic identity in the Catholic Church. Ultimately, the Catholic Church provided a degree of spiritual agency for those who incorporated Catholic practices to fit into their lives. For the most part, rural Catholic slaveholders in South Louisiana encouraged Catholicism among their slaves.

Surprisingly, some blacks, especially free women of color, and some slaves, did indeed incorporate Catholicism into their daily lives. For historians endeavoring to tell the stories of the women, the slaves, native Americans or the settlers who had no means to record their histories and religious beliefs in written form, the work of discovering and recreating their world becomes a complicated task of sifting through church and court records.

In spite of the difficulties in recreating the lives of women and slaves through the words of their husbands or masters, their words often reveal that women and slaves helped to construct the development of Catholicism in rural antebellum Louisiana. Religion, especially during the early nineteenth century, became a venue for black women to express their identities and even create power where little seemed to be.

In the rural southeastern parishes of Louisiana, St. John the Baptist, St. Charles and St. James, free and enslaved men and women also adopted and adapted Catholicism to fit into their lives.

Free women in St. Charles Parish, like the members of the Sisters of the Holy Family, utilized the role of the Church in their communities to expand their social identities and exhibit their economic resources. Several free women of color donated domestic goods to the local priest, for example, expressing religious sensibilities and financial wherewithal.

Other free and enslaved Catholics in the river parishes aided priests during Mass as sacristans or assisted with the administration of sacraments in private homes, inviting the Catholic Church into the most intimate moments of their lives. Enslaved parishioners changed the nature of Catholicism in rural parishes by melding Catholic rituals with African and African-American spirituality. Slaves in St. Charles Parish shared their knowledge of medicinal herbs and folk practices with the local priest, changing the way that he and they approached the connections between spiritual and physical healing.

Most histories of black Catholicism in Louisiana focus either on the early development of French missionaries in the Mississippi River delta or on the relationships between Catholic officials, slaveholding parishioners, and enslaved persons in New Orleans. Both historians and nineteenth-century observers are prone to note how slaves and masters could sit in the same pews, receive communion from the same ciborium as confirmed Catholics with the same religious rights, then return to social, political, and economic relationships marked by inequality.

The sacramental and civil records of St. Charles, St. John the Baptist, St. James, and New

Orleans parishes, reveal how African-American parishioners, especially free women of color, utilized their local Catholic churches as community centers to worship, to trade, and to communicate with fellow black and white parishioners. Enslaved men and women also engaged parish priests in meaningful spiritual and economic exchange, some attaining property and even freedom through their association with the Catholic Church. Their economic and social agency, to be sure, was not unlimited or unequivocally sanctioned by Catholic or local political officials: reception of communion on Sunday did not mean equal rights on Monday.

Yet the Catholic Church, particularly in the river parishes outside New Orleans, proved a way for many African Americans to understand the world around them - whether they were enslaved or free - the Catholic religion in St. Charles, St. John the Baptist and St. James Parishes was a contextualized vehicle to further economic and social objectives for people of color.

Below: Alexander Hamilton, quoted in Liliane Creté, *Daily Life in Louisiana, 1815-1830*, trans. Patrick Gregory (Baton Rouge: Louisiana State University Press, 1981).

Robert C. Reinders, "*The Churches and the Negro in New Orleans, 1850-1860.*"

Pierre Landry, *From Slavery to Freedom* (unpublished memoirs) in Charles B. Rousseve, *The Negro in Louisiana*

"To most American visitors of the time, interracial worship marked the Catholic churches of antebellum New Orleans and the river parishes as unique." Many visitors, from foreign lands, to the city during the eighteenth and early nineteenth centuries observed integrated seating arrangements, contrasting the Catholic churches in South Louisiana to their experiences with segregated churches in other southern and northern congregations.

One observer praised the conduct of priests and parishioners, writing that "the prince and peasant, the slave and master, kneel before the same altar in temporary oblivion of all worldly distinctions. They come in but one character, that of sinners."

Frederick Law Olmsted agreed, noting that the interracial seating in Louisiana's Catholic churches rendered some religious equality within the pews despite hierarchical social and economic relationships outside church walls. On plantations and in towns outside the city, interracial worship was common. As early French and Spanish missionary priests administered sacraments to the free and the enslaved, the Catholic churches in the river parishes around New Orleans continued to serve both black and white parishioners. Apparent regard for the religious lives of all parishioners linked urban and rural Catholic churches in Louisiana.

Tannenbaum, Slave and Citizen: *The Negro in the Americas* (New York: Alfred A. Knopf, 1947) Black Code, Articles II, III, V, VIII, and XI, in American Catholics and Slavery: 1789-1866

"According to the Church, slaves, as rational human beings, were capable of understanding the teachings of the Church and preparing their souls for salvation. The Code Noir, issued by the Catholic King of France to ensure that French colonists in the New World practiced Roman Catholicism, reinforced Catholic teachings on slavery."

"The Code ordered that all slaveholders baptize their slaves and that slaveholders observe Sundays and holy days by forbidding slaves to work in the fields. All priests needed the permission of the owner for slave marriages, and colonial law required slaveholders to bury baptized slaves in ground consecrated by Catholic priests.

Placing Louisiana under the specifications set forth in the Siete Partidas, Spanish officials in colonial Louisiana maintained the religious rights of slaves and extended the rights of free people of color. While continuing to follow the basic provisions of the French Code, French and Spanish Capuchins could now perform interracial marriages between free people of color and whites. Marriages between slaves, was technically allowed by the Code and required by the Siete Partidas, but few slave owners encouraged slaves to marry in the Church."

Capuchin missionaries had established St. Charles Parish and the German Coast in the mid-1720s. Note that the family of Etienne Daigle and Adam Schexnayder were both living in St. Charles

Parish near Taft in the late 1720s. Many years before constructing a permanent church in New Orleans, Capuchins maintained a mission in Taft along the Mississippi River to serve the German and French families lured by John Law to settle above New Orleans on the German Coast.

Perhaps as early as 1721, the settlers of the German Coast attended a temporary missionary chapel called St. Jean des Allemands (St. John of the Germans) on the left bank of the river, near modern day Taft. A more permanent log church dedicated to St. Charles Borromeo was erected in 1740 on the opposite bank of the river.

In 1806, about twenty years after the McCutchon family built Ormond, a frame church, painted a dull red, replaced the original log structure. A series of French and some Spanish Capuchin priests served the parish throughout the antebellum period, and well into the early twentieth century, many of the priests of the Little Red Church were native French speakers.

Father Francis Basty, the church's last native French speaker as well as the church's longest serving priest, oversaw the construction of the current St. Charles Borromeo Church and school complex in the 1920s and 1930s. St. Charles Borromeo Church: 250th Anniversary Celebration, 1723-1973

End of Excerpts

The towns of Edgard and Lucy, for example, developed around St. John the Baptist Church, and several small hamlets grew around St. James Church. This movement west along the river is the start of the building of the great plantations along the river road.

Slavery in Louisiana, however, was unique. In the first place, it arrived nearly a century later than on the East Coast. In the second place, it initially fared badly. Between 1719 and 1731, the French who colonized Louisiana imported 6,000 Africans. Slaves soon composed 60 percent of the population. But disease, starvation, and the work they encountered hacking plantations from virgin forest led most to flee into the nearby wilderness and up on the East Coast.

Many renegade "maroon" settlements took root in the lower Mississippi Valley, further north, with native Americans. In 1729 the French stopped importing slaves into South Louisiana. With most of their fledgling colony in shambles, they made rudimentary moves to pacify their remaining bondsmen. Louisiana's Code Noir specified that slave families were to be kept together when possible and all slaves instructed in the teachings of the Catholic Church. Children younger than 14 were not to be separated from their parents. In addition, any master who fathered children by his own slave was to lose both slave and child; they would be sold to benefit the local hospital and never allowed freedom.

Slave Trade and Slavery in Early Louisiana

Excerpts from
Slave and Citizen: The Negro in the Americas,
Frank Tannenbaum, Alfred Knopf, 1947

"The domestic slave trade transplanted approximately 1 million slaves from what was called the Upper South (primarily Kentucky, Tennessee, Virginia, Maryland, District of Columbia, North Carolina) to what was once called the Southwest (Alabama, Mississippi, Western Georgia, Louisiana, Texas, Arkansas) between 1808, the year which the United States effectively abolished the importation of slaves and 1865, the year the Civil War ended.

Most people think of slave traders moving slaves overland in coffles. However, there was another method of transporting slaves, and that was by the coastal waterways from as far North as Boston along the Eastern Seaboard all the way to New Orleans, a trip that typically took four to six weeks. The coastwise manifests, Record Group 36 of the United States Customs Service, document this aspect of the transshipment of slaves.

That so many African Americans were sold South or transplanted South with their owners, many of whom moved their whole plantations, has implications for African American history and the domestic slave trade – two phenomenon that occurred at the same time, involving the same people but remembered differently, written about differently and obviously experienced differently.

It is utterly strange that there is tremendous silence in the oral history about such a huge migration of people. The owners were Northerners, mostly from New England. The customs officers at New Orleans apparently took their jobs seriously, often noting these inconsistencies and often reflecting their suspicion that the slaves being brought were arriving from Africa rather than from a location in the United States. This may account for the seeming difference between Northern blacks and Southern blacks."

In some cases, the customs officers in New Orleans indicates that the slaves faced a roll call. Note that the parties to the shipment all had to sign the manifests declaring that they were in compliance with the US law prohibiting further importation of slaves after January 1, 1808.

The first paragraph of the manifests typically contained these words:

"Manifest of Negroes, Mulattos and Persons of Color, taken on board the (Name of ship) whereof (name of ship master), burthen (ship tonnage), to be transported to the Port of (name of Port) for the purpose of being sold or disposed of as slaves or to be held to service or labor."

Note: held to the service of labor. It seems most of the slaves were actually owned by Northerners who brought their property South so they could be "contracted" for labor on Southern Plantations, while not actually being owned by Southerners.

The declaration at the bottom of the manifest which had to be signed by the ship master and the lawful agent or owner of the slaves read:

"I, (Name) do solemnly, sincerely, and truly swear to the best of my knowledge and belief that the persons above, specified were not imported or brought into the United States, since the first day of January, eighteen-hundred and eight, and that under the Laws of the State of (name of state), they are held to serve or labor as slaves, so help me God. Collectors1 Office signature at the Port of Departure and signature of owner/agent."

Upon arrival at New Orleans, the customs officer had to inspect the slaves and verify the content of the manifests after which he affixed his signature. In one case, the New Orleans customs officer made a long set of notes (Entry 404), reproduced below:

"I have examined the within named and described slaves, and found them to agree with the general manifest, with the following exceptions:

1. Sam White (No. 12) appears to me to be a full blooded mulatto but in other respects agrees with his description in the manifest.

2. George Washington (No. 35) appears not to be quite black: I should judge him to be three fourths, or, if such a mixture be possible, four-fifths black.

Permitted to land except that Monday and Hannah appear to be "New Negroes from the Gold Coast three years since." 11th February "Examined the slaves described in the annexed manifest. Find them to agree. Monday and Hannah in this manifest have the appearance of New Negroes from the Coast - they cannot speak English."

Or consider the very first entry wherein "A New negro man with a collar round his neck with Hugh Young writ upon it" was brought in from Charleston in 1807 and for whom freight of $30 was paid.

"Manifest of slaves belonging to R. Richardson of Savannah and brought overland from the state of Georgia into West Florida for the purpose of being transported from there to the state of Louisiana and now shipped as passengers on board the steam ship Robert Fulton, Timothy Bannard, Master ... from Pensacola for New Orleans. Owner is Richard Richardson, Connecticut."

End of Excerpt

You should be happy to note that of all the owners who had to be listed by law as engaged in the shipping of slaves, no Daigles or Schexnayders were on any list covering the years of shipment. There are early records from St. Charles Borromeo Church of a few farm hands possibly being owned by the Daigles and the Schexnayders as farm hands but no records of slaves. Records in Lafayette Parish indicate the slaves were freed in the very early 1800s but remained with the families. It was in 1808 that the United States banned, by penalty of imprisonment, the shipment of slaves into the United States.

Slaves of Slaves

Data taken from various sources

There are few aspects in history that confound our present understanding of slavery as much as African American slave owners, though they existed for almost the entire history of slavery in North America. Slavery in Louisiana was unique to Louisiana. Slaves and masters established a bond between the families as witnessed by the early release of slaves long before the Civil War in Louisiana, and the fact that many slaves did not want to leave the confines of the plantation or farm or the family that owned them.

The 1830 U.S. census documented 3,600 "Negro slaveholders." Like thousands of free Negroes of her era, Marie Therese Coincoin "saw no conflict between her own love of freedom and the slave system in which she lived. Slavery not only existed in the white world she knew, but in the [Native American] world with which frontier whites rubbed shoulders, as well as in the "African land" of her parents, of which she had only heard stories. Slavery existed in Africa by Africans, as well as in America. Free blacks worked scores of slaves on their own plantations, and often bought, sold and employed them like their white counterparts.

By 1810, Coincoin's seven sons had accumulated 58 slaves, according to Mills' census research in "The Forgotten People." Of the 259 households in their census area, only 166 owned any slaves at all. In the census of the time, no white people owned more slaves than did blacks own slaves.

Nonwhite slave owners, however, were in somewhat of a bind. If they treated their slaves too leniently, they risked being lumped by their white neighbors into a lower racial class. If they treated them too severely, they risked feeding the widespread white suspicion that blacks were incapable of exercising the judgment and responsibilities of freedom.

Another problem existed in South Louisiana. Early Africans married Native Americans and later the Spanish and French, and color changed; thus, the "mullato," "sabine," and "Mari" classes were formed. Dark-skinned blacks did not want to associate with light-skinned blacks, and mullatos and sabines formed their own communities. Many of these communities still exist today. Mullatos in Lacombe. Sabines in Dulac. Mari's in Charenton. In modern day New Orleans there is still a distinction between the light-skinned blacks and the dark-skinned blacks.

A 1974 study of slave life, based on the 1860 census, found slave housing and conditions in South Louisiana somewhat crude but more than adequate and far less crowded than in most of the North and other areas of the South. Many slaves were furnished firearms to hunt with indicating a trust between owner and slave.

Slavery in Louisiana was unique but it must be understood that slavery was not just a Southern situation. Slaves were predominately brought South by Northern slave owners to work as contract labor on the large plantations. The practice of slavery was not unique to the South, but slavery in Louisiana, due to conditions and circumstances which only existed in Louisiana, caused slavery in Louisiana to be unique.

The renowned Civil War author and historian, Professor Donald Frazier, documents the historical fact that the great South Louisiana plantations were owned, not by native Louisianans, but by rich Northerners from New York and Boston. The slaves transported South to work on these plantations were part of a regular trade between the Northeast businessmen and the Northerners who owned the large plantations along the river. The slaves were essentially contracted labor. The areas around Opelousas, Caddo and Bossier parishes is where succession was pushed.

According to Professor Frazier, the Union armed the local Indian tribes and paid them to fight a guerilla war against the Confederates. The largest area of fighting was the Atchafalaya Basin. As in modern times, the value of the Mississippi River was understood, and from the beginning of the war the Union wanted control of the Mississippi River.

Some sources used are: Black Code, Articles II, III, V, VIII, and XI, in American Catholics and Slavery: 1789-1866

THE SCHEXNAYDERS
The Settling of the River Parishes

John Law

John Law made a deal to settle Louisiana. He circulated thousands of pamphlets. Thousands of Germans signed up, but most of them died and only a few hundred made it to the New World.

John Law and the Company of the Indies settled Germans along the Mississippi River in present-day St. Charles and St. John the Baptist Parishes in 1720. When the Company of the Indies folded in 1731, the Germans were released from their obligation and became independent land owners.

The Germans were an important source of produce for the small town of New Orleans, founded in 1718 just a few years before their arrival.

John Law, a Scottish economist, was an innovator in banking, investment, speculation, and in the use of paper money. In the few years before 1721, he founded the Mississippi Company using the influence from his French governmental post. This company was later absorbed into the Company of the Indies. Part of the company's scheme was to provide the Mississippi Delta with colonists, and thus German and other immigrants were courted. For the Germans, thousands of pamphlets were circulated and thousands of them signed on, but most of them died either on the disease-ridden journey or from hostile Native Americans in their attempt to establish colonies upriver at the Arkansas Post. There were further hardships from lack of supplies due to the Company's amateurish support. The survivors made their way to the beaches of Biloxi to regroup, to be led later by the Swedish-German Karl D'Arensbourg to fertile land along the river that is now known as St. Charles and St. John the Baptist parishes. Settling there successfully in 1721, the colonists began supplying much-needed sustenance to the soldiers and functionaries in the struggling encampment of New Orleans, which had been founded in 1718, just a few years before their arrival. The Company's bankruptcy in 1731 released the settlers from their servitude status, but they continued supplying New Orleans by selling their surplus harvest, and were instrumental in the city's growth into and throughout the 1800s, supplying timber as well as staples.

The German and Acadian Coast
By Jay Schexnaydre

"The German and Acadian Coasts are not "coasts" as in "land along the seashore of an ocean." A coast by definition is "the land near the shore," but in this case the shore is the land along the Mississippi River. During the 18th and 19th centuries, the term *coast* was used to describe the distinct settlements situated just above New Orleans along the Mississippi River's edge. (The origin of the word "coast" came from the French noun *le côte* – the side, of a box, a river, or bayou, and from this we have The Gulf Coast, the Acadian Coast and the German Coast. The origins of the word "parish" also came from the naming of territories from smaller settlements, so as the territories grew the church influenced the term "parish.") There are naturally two coasts. The left coast or bank was the land on your left side if traveling downriver (the east bank), and the right coast or bank was the land on your right-hand side (the west bank)."

It's helpful to look at the history of the great Mississippi river. Going back to 1539, 700 men under De Soto landed at Tampa Bay and marched across the present states of Florida, Alabama, and Mississippi. In 1541 they reached the Mississippi River above the mouth of the Arkansas River, where De Soto died. Led by Moscoso, they moved downriver, and in 1542 were the first Europeans to see the area now known as St. James Parish. They were seeking gold, and since no gold was found they abandoned the area.

During John Law's later colonization era, two tribes of Indians had lived on the west bank (that

was to become the German Coast), the Washas &
and Chawashas, but they were better known by
their local French *patois* names: Ouacha –
"unknown" – and Chaouachas – "raccoon place
people." In the early 1700s, New Orleans founder
Jean-Baptiste le Moyne de Bienville, working for the
French Mississippi Company, moved the tribes six
miles above New Orleans and to the east side of the
river. Further south and west were the tribes of the
Chickasaws, Chocktaws, Yemases, Bayougoulas,
and Houmas Indians.

Parts of John Law's colonization scheme had
come to fruition after many difficulties, and
eventually the German and Acadian settlers were
well established along this part of the river north of
New Orleans.

In the 1750s, in what is present day St.
James Parish, there were large tracts of land along
the west bank of the river that the colonial
government granted to individuals wanting to raise
cattle. (*Vacherie* in French means cattle ranch or
cow shed). These grants were later subdivided into
smaller lots with individual owners, which then
became parts of large plantations.

The German and Acadian Coasts are named
for the first European settlers to be established
along the shores of the river. The First German
Coast was located in modern-day St. Charles Parish
along the west bank of the river between the
modern communities of Killona and Taft, which
were settled by Germans as early as the 1720s. As
this settlement eventually grew, others began to
appear further upriver in present day St. John the
Baptist Parish, near Edgard, and thus the west
bank of the parish became known as the Second

German Coast. The population grew over the years, and the settlement was dispersed along the entire coast on both sides of the river, and thus St. Charles and St. John the Baptist Parish collectively became known as the German Coast.

Francois Michel Schexnayder & Louisa Zeringue

The area of the Germans along the river was called Carlstein. The area between Luling, Edgard and Wallace referred to a site on the west bank of the river near the present site of the St. John the Baptist and St. Charles Parish line. This is literally within a few thousand feet of our (Daigle, Schexnayder) present day land in Vacherie.

The First Acadian Coast was established along the Mississippi River in St. James Parish near the St. James Catholic Church. These Acadians, later to become known as Cajuns, were exiled from Acadia (now Nova Scotia, New Brunswick, and Prince Edward Island, Canada) beginning in 1755 by the British. By the 1760s, many of the Acadians had made their way to the haven of French (later Spanish) Catholic Louisiana. Later, as other exiled Acadians received word from family and friends in Louisiana, many of those in France and along the eastern U.S. seaboard traveled to Louisiana to reunite with family and establish homes as well. However, more land was needed, and the Second Acadian Coast was founded further upriver in today's Ascension Parish. Thus St. James and part of Ascension comprised the Acadian Coast. Anyone tracing their family ancestry through the German and Acadian coasts can tell you that many of the Germans and Acadians themselves did not remain in their original settlements. Many moved up and down the river, searching in different locations for better farming or other opportunities, intermarrying as they went. Now many of the German names are found among the French names in St. James, and Acadian names are found in St. John and St. Charles.

These areas were not solely settled by Germans and Frenchman, in fact many of the "Germans" came from the bilingual Alsace-Lorraine region of France and some from Bohemia, Hungary, Austria, Switzerland and Belgium. For the most part they were natives of Alsace, the Palatinate, and Baden. Some had names like Schexnayder. Louisiana also saw many non-Acadian French who came directly from France, the Caribbean Islands, and from other parts of Canada, namely Québec – some had names like Daigle. Others were Spanish, and there were many Africans, most brought as slaves from West Africa. But a good representation of Les Gens de Couleur Libres (Free People of Color) could also be found along the coasts, many who had migrated from the Caribbean, others born in Louisiana.

Human nature being what it is, over the years all of these groups would eventually intermarry and form many large "families" of people all related somewhere along the line, perhaps ten generations back.

Chances are if you're not someone's cousin, then one of your cousins or your spouse may be related to them. At this point it should be mentioned that because the Germans would soon be outnumbered by their French speaking counterparts, the Germanic languages spoken by these first settlers eventually died out, to be replaced by French.

These settlements were founded in the Lower Delta of the Mississippi, which over millions of years has deposited much sediment to form most of current southeast Louisiana. Along the banks of the river, this sediment formed natural levees, an average elevation of about 10 feet above sea level. The land behind the levee would gradually slope from anywhere from 1/2 to 2 miles into the cypress swamps where the elevation was only a few inches above sea level. Each spring, the river would often overflow its banks and, in most cases, a crevasse would form and break the natural levee, inundating the land with a fresh deposit of fertile sediment. Needless to say, this process has provided the Lower Delta with some of the richest, most fertile land in the world; however, this process would also cause many problems for the 18th century settlers who attempted to permanently establish their homes here.

These settlers attempted to protect themselves from the crevasses and flooding of the river by improving the natural levees and building man-made ones (known elsewhere as dikes). In dividing the land for settlement, the colonial government officials employed the French long-lot system, whereby each landowner was given a parcel with a narrow river frontage. The parcels would then extend parallel to each other and perpendicular from the river back towards the swamps. Each landowner was required to maintain the portion of the levee on their property, and they even owned the land between the river and the levee, known as the *batture*.

Today, the terms German and Acadian Coasts will seldom be heard in conversation to describe the parishes of St. Charles, St. James or St. John the Baptist. They are unfortunately used to explain our area only in historical terms. Many of today's residents of these areas are unaware of the terms originally applied to their parishes. Collectively today, the tri-parishes are popularly known as the River Parishes, which implies those along the Mississippi River between New Orleans and Baton Rouge.

The terms "east bank" and "west bank" are in wide use to distinguish which side of the river one is located. And not a day goes by that someone doesn't say "across the river" or in the past, *l'autre bord du fleuve* to refer to the residents or the communities on the opposite bank from themselves.

Elina Plantation is located in Welcome, Louisiana. In the early 1800s, this area offered refuge to the Alabama Indians, then to the exiled Acadians, and in the years following the Civil war it became the home of former plantation slaves who joined together and purchased tracts of land with colorful names such as Moonshine, Burton Lane, Chatman, Freetown, Hymel, and Welcome.

Information provided from State of Louisiana History, St. Charles, St. John the Baptist & St. James Parishes

The Early German Settlers

In St. Charles Parish, the first German Coast was the area along the river, and Des Allemands was the area around the lake. As we've seen in the history of the coasts along the Mississippi, the settlers were German farmers who contracted with John Law and his West Indies company to undertake the cultivation of farms in the lush wilderness of Louisiana. They came in family units of parents, children, and other relatives. Having voluntarily contracted to come to Louisiana, once they departed Europe they never looked back. Even with the unbelievable hardships they endured in Louisiana, they never yearned to return to their homeland.

These eighteenth-century settlers arrived in three groups; the first arrived between 1720 and 1738 and included the families of the Schexnayders, Segschneider, Edelmeiers, Zweigs, Heidels, and Himmels. Being yeoman farmers, they sought the rich farmland along the Mississippi River. They settled primarily above New Orleans in St. Charles Parish, On the west bank of the river having found deforested land which had been the site of vacated Tensas Indian villages.

The early years were a struggle with unfamiliar elements, disease, and famine, but gradually as the French joined in (Daigles arrived in 1717 or 1720), the semi-tropical jungle of St. Charles Parish was pushed back from the banks of the river and replaced by cultivated fields. Indigo was the primary crop during these times, but was replaced later in the mid-1700s as sugar cane became the primary agricultural crop.

From the records of these early years, it's apparent that the legal scribes gave up on trying to record the names of the German families in favor of simply assigning them French names – with the exception of Schexnayder, which remained on the logs and legal documents of the period in many diverse spellings that we still see today.

As a side note however, the family was not known as Schexnayder, but rather as "Albert," the name of the head of the Schexnayder clan, Albert Schexnayder. It is recorded that Albert and Schexnayder refer to the same family, so there is no confusion.

In later years the Acadian family of Antoine Albert (O-bear) settled in the same area, and therefore the Schexnayders had to resume using their proper name.

The spelling of Schexnayder was, at one time or another in Louisiana, Schexnaydre, **Segschneider**, Sexchneyder, Sexnaidre, Snydre, Sixtailleur, Seckshneyder, Secxnauder, Scheixneydre, Chisnaitre, Cheixnaydre, and Hexnaider.

Civil Records of St. Charles and St. John the Baptist Parish. Book 6 – 1776

Church Document, Henri Albert Schexnayder

"Inventory of the Community Property of the late Henri Albert Schexnayder and his wife Marianne Edelmeier. Henri Albert died January 4, 1776 (Act #144) and Bellile orders an inventory of the property. The inventory was taken by unknown person of St. Charles Parish, in the presence of the widow, Marianne Edelmeier, Andre, Henri Albert and Andre' Aidelmayre, son-in-law of the decedent, married to Catherine Schexnayder; and Josette and Julienne Schexnayder.

"His sons Jean-Baptist and Adam and his daughter Catherine are not present. Schexnayder was married twice; first to Madelaine Vique and second, to Marianne Aidelmayder. [Document No. 214]

"Partition of the succession of the late Albert Schexnayder. (Act #151) Bellile is charged with the responsibility of partitioning the succession between his widow, Marianne Aidelmayre (widow, by her first marriage, of André, Henry-Albert, George, Ambroise, Jean-Baptist, Adam, Marguerite, Catherine, Josette and Julienne. Following the death of Madelaine Bernard, Schexnayder had an inventory of the community property made, dated March 5, 1767. Community property amounted to 14,335 livres and was partitioned between the widower and his children. Following that,

Schexnayder married Marianne Aidelmayre and had one son, Epiphany.

"Bellile is ordered to partition the estate of Albert Schexnayder among the children of his first marriage and that of his second marriage. The succession amounts to 8,182 piastres with deductions of one half of the succession of his first wife which came to Schexnayder; 1,433 piastres which is to be partitioned among the children of his first marriage.

A deduction of 425 piastres which Marianne Aidelmayre brought to her second marriage from the succession of her first husband, André Belsom. (André Belsom and Marianne Aidelmayre had seven children) "The total deductions (not all listed) amount to 3,166 piastres. The succession is valued at 5,016 piastres.

"To Marianne Aidelmayre, is partitioned 2,507 piastres and the remaining 2,507 piastres are to be divided among the Schexnayder's children of both marriages. To this amount is to be added the inheritance of the children of the first marriage from their mother. Hence, each one of them receives 501 piastres and Epiphany, child of the second marriage receives 358 piastres."

As you can see, confusion started early in the Schexnayder family and has carried through to today. They just have too many of them.

Note: Civil Records of St. Charles and St. John the Baptist Parishes and St. Charles Borromeo Church

TRAVELS IN THE RIVER PARISHES
Vacherie
From the book, "Vacherie"
by Elton J. Oubre

"Vacherie is a crevasse, which is a smaller version of the formation of a delta in both size and time, an overflow where the river breaks out of its channel. The Vacherie Crevasse from the river to where Pointe Aux Herbes (Cypress Point) juts out into Lake Des Allemands was one of many areas where the river broke out of its banks and overflowed to the Gulf. Interestingly, the river today is in the same position as it was 2,000 years ago. The main overflow was at the present site of Donaldsonville, and formed Bayou Lafourche. The communities of Luling, Boutte, Paradis, Des Allemands, and Bayou Gauche were formed from the Vacherie Crevasse (Le Coteau De France). The dating of Indian artifacts found on the banks of Bayou Lafourche and Les Coteau De France provided the information to accurately chart the course of the river overflow."

Vacherie's history is linked to modern times, and St. John the Baptist and St. James Parishes are the site of Valcour Aime's plantation, the present Laura Plantation. Tabiscania, the early site where the Indians lived, developed a large complex of mounds in Vacherie called Shell Hill.

Besides Shell Hill, it's interesting that at Vacherie shells are found at the tip of Point d'Herbes (Fausse Point) and along Ti-bayou at Aristide Becnel's camp on Brazan Canal, as well as on the levees of Simon Schexnayders crawfish ponds. Present day maps of family land at Vacherie show the area of the crawfish ponds, and in fact, when I first saw this I went to the area to look for them, but they have long since been covered by the swamp. This area is at the back of the family property, just off Hwy. 3127. Tulane archeologists have taken measurements and recordings of the area and have referred the site to a state archeologist at LSU for research and excavation.

Vacherie, St. James Parish History, by E.J. Oubre 2002

The Shifting Deltaic Coast – Weinstein / Gagliano
The Indian Tribes of North America – Swanson
A Comparative View of French Louisiana – Brasseau
Carte Particulaire Du Cours Du Fleuve Mississipy – Broutin

The Madstone of Vacherie

Information Provided by Mrs. Eddie Oubre
The Madstone was given to the Gravois family by an Indian whom the family had nursed back to health after a long illness. The stories told about the stone are those of miraculous cures through "treatments" with it. There were treatments for snake bites, mad dogs, and many types of infections, and people came from far away to seek its healing effects. Doctors and scientists studied the stone and were never able to explain its miraculous healing powers. Applied to a bite or infected area, the stone would adhere like a strong magnet until all the poison was removed. Hundreds

of people have been cured by its strange healing powers.

The Madstone in its original form was about 3 inches long and about 3/4 inches in diameter; it was white and was said to have been removed from the heart of an albino deer. It was dropped and broken into three pieces, but the healing powers still remain. The Gravois family has the stone. One of their children, Edgar Gravois, was the husband of Agnes Schexnayder, and they were the parents of Mary Lou and Linda.

Plantations of Garyville

Information from *Precious Gems of Memory*, Dr. Gerald Keller

With the failure of indigo, St. John the Baptist turned its attention to sugar cane. The production of sugar during these times carried great risks. It was a commodity that required an immense amount of labor and heavy financial investment. Plantation owners turned to the supply of slave labor, which was being brought into the area from the northeast United States.

Amour Plantation - Thomas D'Aquin Bougeois owned and operated Amour during the Civil War, when the mill was destroyed.

Emilie Plantation - Built by George Chauffe in 1840, the ownership passed to Cyprien Chauffe, and later the original house burned. The new house was built in 1882 by Adelard Millet for Leonce Chauff. In the early 1920s, the house was purchased by Sidney and Lauren Levet, and recently the house was sold to Carl and Geri Broussard Baloney.

Emilie Plantation

Angelina Plantation - James Godbery was the original owner in 1860, then W. B. Gloomfield acquired ownership several years later, and finally the Trosclairs became the owners up to now.

Glencoe Plantation - Francois Perilloux was the owner in 1883. Leon Graugnard sold the plantation to the Southern Cypress Company, the forerunner of the Lyon Lumber Company. Currently the town of Garyville occupies the site of the old Glencoe Plantation.

Hope Plantation - Hope Plantation House was once part of a plantation known as Esperance, a French word meaning Hope. The house was built in 1828 by Honore Landreaux and Joseph Lavergne. In 1870, Ozeme Labiche bought the house, and in 1912 sold it to the Babin brothers. The Millet family moved to Garyville in 1923 and rented the house and operated a dairy until the late 1950s. In 1937 the house was sold to Walter Stebbins, who allowed the Millets and their eleven children to stay on. In 1940, Leo Millet was killed, and later that year Mrs. Millet bought the home from Mr. Stebbins. Mrs. Millet died on August 23,

1985. Her descendants still own the house and property.

Late in the 1990s, a town reunion (mostly people who lived on the river) was held at Hope Plantation. Belle and I attended. The first town reunion was held a few years earlier, which was predominantly people from the back, but everyone attended. What was especially notable about these reunions was the fact that they were attended by people from Garyville now living in other parts of the country, which in my estimation is a tribute to the closeness of the community and its people.

San Francisco Plantation - Records indicate that the plantation was built in 1820 by a "free man of color," Elisee Rillieux. He sold the house in 1830 to Edmond Marmillion, and the plantation was a thriving sugar cane business. In 1859, Valsin Marmillion gave the house its name, "Sans Frusquin," a popular French expression meaning "one's all" or "reduced to one's last cent." Stories say the elaborate house consumed all the family's wealth.

The architecture of the manor is French, but it is often called "Steamboat Gothic," and by that name became the subject of a novel by Francis Parkinson Keyes. In 1904, management of the plantation was handed over to Sidney Levet and John M. Ory, and as time passed Claude then Carl Levet managed the sugar cane farms. I played in and around the house as a young boy; Carl and I grew up together.

In 1973, the plantation and sugar mill was sold to Marathon Oil Company, which owns it today. The sugar mill was dismantled and shipped to Panama, where it is still in operation.

Above: San Francisco Planting and Manufacturing Company

Farm workers on San Francisco Plantation (Courtesy of Carl L. Lever Family)

Information from Precious Gems of Memory, St. John the Baptist Parish, Dr. Gerald Keller

Garyville

Plantations existed before Garyville was founded in 1903 by the Lyon Lumber Company, and in fact the town was made up of three of them, Glencoe and two adjoining plantations, Emelie and Hope. German, French, and Spanish settled this area, and in the mid 1800s the Italians found their way to Garyville; in that time, the town had its own version of Little Italy, known then as Rapatedo (now referred to as Bourgeois Town), but plantations were for the most part the center of economic activity. Before the introduction of burlap sacks and rail tank cars, sugar – in its liquid crystal form – had to be shipped in wooden barrels, and cooperages, or barrel making, thrived between 1860 and the early 1900s. The Perilloux family, in partnership with Albert Millet, owned a barrel making business that produced 12,000 barrels a year.

The Lyon Lumber Company was the largest cypress mill in the world at one time, and when the cypress was exhausted, this enterprise would go on to become the second largest pine mill in the world, and at its peak, the mill employed at least 1,200 workers. Agriculture dominated St. John the Baptist Parish as a whole, but timber dominated Garyville. Due to the logging of cypress, the residents of Manchac, Ruddock, Galva, and Frenier maintained a very close relationship with the people of Garyville. The post office at Manchac used the address of Akers, so the town of Manchac was legally Akers.

Lyon Lumber Company in Garyville

The Great Depression dealt a blow to the town, and Garyville changed forever. In 1931, Lyon Lumber closed its doors and laid off over 1,000 workers. The company moved to Oregon's vast western forest, and Garyville died.

In 1932, Walter J. Stebbins bought the lumber company and Stebbins was born, a full service lumber yard.The original Lyon Lumber

Company building is still standing, but precariously. It had become a museum, but was closed after several years due to a general lack of interest.

In its early years, Garyville was a true company town with all the amenities; a post office, the Big Store, the four room Garyville School, a community club, the Magnolia Hotel, the Garyville Hotel and Library, the Gary State Bank and the Garyville Movie Theater, the first in the parish. In 1907 St. Hubert's Catholic Church was built. Saint Hubert is the patron saint of hunters. Garyville also had an automobile dealership, an ice cream parlor, a druggist, a Masonic hall, baseball parks, and even a tennis court. Baseball legend Ty Cobb owned a house in Garyville.

Precious Gems from Faded Memories, Gerald Keller, Lisa Keller, Darroch Watson

History of St. John the Bapist Parish, Rt. Rev. Magr. Jean Eyraud, Donald Millet

Monica Family

Magnolia Hotel in Garyville (Courtesy of Carl Monica)

Garyville Hotel and Library (Courtesy of Carl Monica)

    – from *History of St. John the Baptist Parish, Hope Haven Press, 1939:*

    "Lyon Cypress Lumber company of Garyville represented the second largest industrial pursuit in the history of St. John the Baptist from 1903 to 1931, when the primary mill closed. Peak employment at the mill was 1,200 workers with payrolls exceeding $1 million annually.

Between the years 1915 and 1931, eighty seven thousand (87,000) rail cars of cypress lumber were shipped around the world from Garyville. Officially, the last cypress log was cut by the mill in 1931 ... W. J. Stebbins, a former manager of Lyon Lumber, purchased the mill in 1931 and began operating the mill as a 'second growth' mill since no first growth cypress remained to be milled." Pine and oak were also milled.

Operations at the mill began to get smaller and smaller. Stebbins continued to operate The Lumber Yard until the 1952 fire. Stebbins, however, continued The Lumber Yard – more of a hardware store – right up to modern times, and the old building still exists, although in very bad condition today. There is a museum in Garyville devoted to the old mill and the cypress industry. Today the museum is also about dead.

Evergreen Plantation

GROWING UP IN GARYVILLE

Picture Taken From Precious Gems from Faded Memories, Dr. Gerald Keller, Lisa-Keller Watson, Darrosch Watson

Thinking back on my growing up in Garyville, I have come to realize that a way of life is long lost, not only to me but to children growing up today. I assumed that rural southern Louisiana was unique, and in particular aspects it was, but when reading Clarence Thomas's *My Grandfather's Son,* I soon realized that growing up in the South was unique in itself. Thomas's experience as a young black man growing up in rural Georgia were in many ways reflections of my own experiences growing up in Garyville.

I didn't know Vernon and Lloyd when I was a young child; they were away in the war when I was born. When they returned from the war they were obviously not interested in a small child, having found better things to do, such as getting married. There were many stories about how strict Dad was with them when they themselves were young, such as taking them to the chicken coop when they misbehaved, but no one has ever verified these stories and they may well be rural legend. My recollections are mostly of Carl, Belle, and Ruth. Dad was certainly tough on me, but I was never taken to the chicken coop. Being the last child, I am sure Mom and Dad had mellowed a great deal when I came along. They were not overly strict with me, but Dad certainly had the cure if I got out of line: a willow switch across the back of the lower legs.

His slow walk across the levee to get the switch, then back, taking his time stripping it with his pocket knife, was worse than the whipping itself. One thing I can say about Dad is that I was at least 30 years old before he accepted me as an adult. I don't know if the problem was mine or just his ways, but fortunately we had many years of a close relationship thereafter.

Vernon and I did not have much time together to develop a real relationship until I was much older. We worked together on the genealogy of the Daigles, and that project did allow us to share a short time to get to know each other. Our infrequent visits at Dad's to fish in the river ponds, or crawfishing on Good Friday, or to his home in Baton Rouge, were not enough to really get to know each other. Also there was a large age difference, and he had his family to raise. But I always respected Vernon and took his advice seriously. Helen was much like Dad's sisters; when you saw her you knew she truly enjoyed seeing you. She is best described as a genuine person.

Carl, Lloyd, Dad, Eddie, Vernon Daigle

Mom and Dad met in Lafayette at the University of Southwest Louisiana (now ULL) in Lafayette. After marrying they moved to Pecan Island in 1920 after being married in Welcome on the Elina plantation. Edward and Leah moved to Garyville from Forked Island in 1923. Mom was college educated in a time when girls seldom went to college, and she became a school teacher. And being a Schexnayder, it's quite interesting to note that the early history of the Daigles and Schexnayders in Louisiana indicate that our two families lived either next to each other or in close proximity.

Both families arrived in Louisiana about the same time (1717 - 1721), more than three decades before the Acadians were brutally evicted from Canada in the *Grand Derangement*.

When Mom and Dad settled in Garyville, Dad became the principal at Garyville Elementary School. They settled in "back" Garyville, which is off the river road. It was in this house where the stories of Vernon and Lloyd being taken to the chicken coop originated. After several years, in 1926 Dad was able to buy some land for farming on the river. He also bought two old houses of solid cypress and took them apart, combining the lumber to build a single house – the one I was born in – in what is now known as "front" Garyville. People were either from the front or the back, and there is a further distinction of being from or going "back the tracks," as if going further back was possible.

Garyville was a fairly large town in its early years, having the largest cypress lumber mill in the world in the late 1800s. But milling cypress became a dying industry after much of the timber had been cut in the late 1800s and early 1900s.

My early life in Garyville revolved around the cypress mill of the Lyon Lumber Company which burned down for the third and last time in 1952, having burned in '26 and '28. I was in the second grade in 1952, and the talk on the bus was about the mill in flames, and everyone wanting to get home fast and then go see the fire. The mill was replaced with a much smaller one that operated in tandem with the Stebbins Lumber Yard, all in close proximity to the original mill. I came along at the end of Garyville's heyday as a mill town, but I remember the large ponds where cypress logs were "floated" before processing. The newly-cut cypress logs were set afloat in the ponds, and only after they sank would the logs be milled to lumber. This lumber would then be stacked to dry in cross fashion for what seemed liked miles, sometimes waiting for several years before being sold. Long after the mill was gone, there were still stacks of lumber with the woods growing up around them.

The old mill ponds are now covered over, but until the early 1980's logs could still be salvaged from those ponds to be milled and then sold at gold prices. In the mid 1980s, the last of the big cypress logs were pulled from the bog. Those ponds also held another treasure, one we had to sneak in to get: turtles, the big loggerheads.

The Mississippi River and the land behind the levee held many treasures and wonderful times. I remember that every year when the river would rise up to the levee, Dad would walk the back side next to the water's edge carrying a pole with a large, barb-less hook, and every now and then he would pull a soft shell turtle from the grass in the shallow water. Soft shell turtle meat is the best. It is mostly white and very tender, and compared in size to hard shell turtles, they had much more meat. Cut into thin strips, battered and fried, the meat was tender and very tasty.

My first experience with a loggerhead turtle was when Mrs. Brady came to the house to summon Dad to her husband's aid. It seems Mr.

Brady had caught a rather large loggerhead, back the levee, and while removing it from the sack the turtle had latched onto his hand. Dad had to cut off the turtle's head, then pry open the jaws to free Mr. Brady's hand.

Mostly Daigles, and some Giffins
and Luminais

Vernon Daigle Family

Clark Giffin Family

Andrew and Art Price, Rene Daigle Jr.,
Matthew Daigle & David Giffin

Mike & Susanne Schexnayder & Helen Daigle

Michele, Amelia & Belle

Dobbins & Mary Lou Guillot

Alexis Price, Cale and Camille Daigle

Gabrial and Camille Daigle

*L to R: Justin Ayers, Jordan Daigle, Edward
Daigle, Leslie Price, Andrew Price Susan Daigle,
Alexis Price, Danielle Ayers*

207

Daniel Price

Ciron Black, Daniel Price, & Big Herman

Nieces & Nephews
& Francis

Clark & Ruth

Andrew Price & friend

Alexis Price & Edward Daigle

Maya Daigle

Edward Daigle & Daniel Price

Martha Ayers & Leslie

Susan & Blythe Daigle

Martha Ayers (Gammie) & Blythe Daigle

Principals Front Row L to R: Aunt Florance (Daigle)
Boudreaux, Aunt Anne (Daigle) Sowar,
Helen Daigle

Blythe Daigle

Mike & Susanne Schexnayder

Casey & Cale Daigle

L to R: Darren, Angelique & Neal Daigle
R to L: Kim, Trey & Lloyd Daigle

My childhood memories are of the river, the
swamps, and Garyville, a town of 800 people.
Everyone knew everyone, black and white, and
there were no problems with race relations. In fact,
none of the young people even thought about it.
But when the sun set, the blacks went to their
homes and the whites did likewise. I truly cannot
remember ever thinking why this was so; it was
just how it was where we lived. Since there were so
few of us kids, we all played together, and of course
the age range was pretty large.

I was sort of a sickly child, having very bad
asthma. Belle took care of me most of the time,
rocking me for hours on end. The remedies I was

given, while failing to cure me, probably gave my body the ability to accept almost anything. I was made to breathe the smoke of burning sassafras leaves. On other occasions I was made to eat petroleum jelly – now *that* was a good one. At least I wasn't made to drink liquified alligator fat ...

Mom, Dad, Belle & Francis

WILLIAM H. AYERS & MARTHA FRANCES BLYTHE
PARENTS OF SUSAN ANN AYERS

Daigle

Edward Daigle Sr

House After Move

Our Car

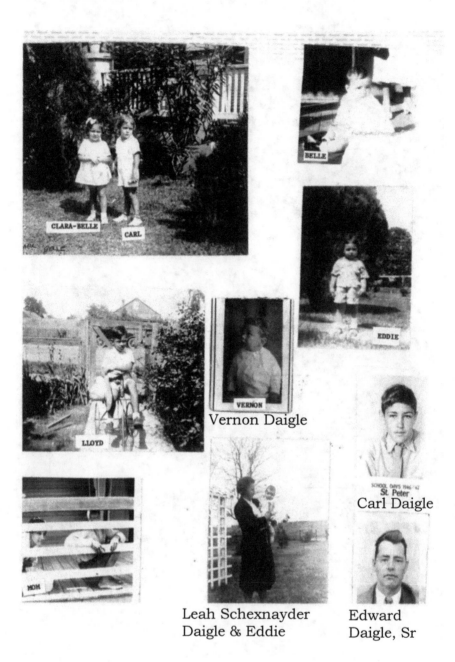

CLARA-BELLE CARL

BELLE

EDDIE

LLOYD

VERNON

Vernon Daigle

SCHOOL DAYS 1946-47
St. Peter

Carl Daigle

MOM

Leah Schexnayder
Daigle & Eddie

Edward
Daigle, Sr

Claribel Daigle

Helen & Vernon

Ruth Ann Daigle Garyville Elementary

Leah Daigle

Eddie   Leah Daigle

Edward Daigle Sr

Edward Sr. & Carl

When I was born, our house was about one-half mile south of where it stands now, closer to the river. It would be well into the river had it remained in its first location. We had a fairly large yard, and on one side of the house was a huge oak tree. It was large enough to have several swings at different levels, and this tree was the gathering place for kids along the river. I don't remember much from this stage of my life, but I do remember when the house was moved to its present site.

When I was little, the levee was very small in comparison to the one that exists now, and the river was trying to take the curve of land on which we lived. In 1947, the levee was moved. I do remember the workers and the teams of mules and oxen which moved all the houses in the curve.

The house was jacked up and the piers removed, then two beams aligned in the direction of the move were placed under the house; logs were spaced out below them. The house was then lowered down. The connections to pull the house were attached to these beams, and six teams of mules or oxen, four to a team, were attached to the other ends and began pulling the house – at least in my memory. This is probably romanticized; Belle remembers tractors moving the house, and maybe the mules and oxen were used to bring the logs from the back around to the front as progress was made. There were many tractors around as the levee was being built and the houses moved. As a log came from the back end (which was actually the front of the house, being pulled back end first), then a log clevis would be attached and a single mule or horse would pull it again to the leading end, and the workers would align it under that end.

The house moved smoothly across the fields for many hours as it rolled about a half mile to its present site.

The next day the house was again jacked up, the logs removed, the piers built, and finally it was settled onto the piers on which it now sits. The cypress timbers used for framing under the house are 12" x 14" beams, and the walls are all 1"x 8" cypress. No sheet rock in those days. Later in the week the mighty oak had to be taken down, so several large holes were drilled, then filled with dynamite and exploded. It took several tries before the tree fell. It was a sad moment for all in the neighborhood.

Some days later I can remember the huge "walking" cranes coming to build the new levee. These large machines couldn't crawl on tracks like cranes do today. They had four large steel pads, and one sat on the ground on each side while the other was lifted and moved about six feet forward, then lowered as the previous pad was rotated

upward. The same thing would happen on the other side. Thus the term "walking" cranes. The pads were necessary to keep the heavy machinery from sinking in the soft ground and mud. It was amazing to see how fast they could build the levee.

We got settled into the new home site. Dad built the three main barns we had at the time: one for hay, one for the wagons and canning, and one for storage of feed corn. Dad always grew tomatoes, potatoes and corn. Some of the corn would be canned for our own use, but most of it was shelled from the cob, some being ground into "crack" corn for chicken feed. Some was for corn meal for cooking, and some of the whole kernels along with the cobs were kept for cow feed.

Everyone had a chicken coop and a barn for hay, horses, wagons and their equipment, and everyone had what we called a "cob barn," which was pronounced "cabarn." Note: "Cabane" in French is a little shack or shed so the association may be the French word rather than the literal corn cob barn. It was for all the corn, fresh included, and the meal went into sacks as it was processed: some as whole kernels for animal feed, some ground into cracked corn for chicken and cow feed. The cobs were kept and fed to the cows with molasses. The term cob barn may only be internal to our family, I'm not sure.

We had a large chicken coop, which housed about 10 laying chickens. In addition to the 10 layers, we had 20 old hens and three happy roosters. Next to the coop we had a three-hole outhouse. It was leftover from earlier days, but it did come in handy at times.

We had two milk cows, two or three heifers, a calf or two, two mules, chickens, pigs (dad got rid of the pigs when the house was moved), several goats, rabbits, two Clydesdales for Dad's plowhorses, and, of course, dogs. My first dog was a collie named Rex. The second was a pot licker my Mom named Jack.

One of my chores was to cut blood weed for the rabbits. Another was to stake the milk cows on the levee in the morning, then bring them into the pasture in the evening. This was a great learning period for me. We had an old dried up milk cow who was red, so "Big Red" she was. One day I decided to give Red a treat and staked her on the levee. It was spring and the red clover was in full bloom. According to Dad, red clover and cows don't go together, and poor Big Red went crazy and died several days later. As I said, this was a great learning period, and this lesson was soundly grilled into me – if it *was* one, because to this day I don't know if red clover is as deadly as Dad made it out to be.

Mom and Dad would go to bed every night after the rosary between 8:30 and 9 and wake up at 5 every morning. The routine was a warm glass of milk or a small glass of red wine before bed and a large glass of warm water first thing in the morning. Dad and I would milk the cows, move them to pasture, then get ready for work and school. Mom would feed the other animals later in the morning after she took care of the house.

I can remember having other chores such as feeding the chickens, and Carl and I participated

Louie & Ethal Normand, Fran and Jeanne

when corn was ground. Dad had a shed behind his garden with one side open to the pasture. Here he mixed his fertilizer, which was comprised of the chicken droppings from under the coop and cow patties (as fresh as possible). When dried, this combination was mixed with a pitchfork and used for the flowers and the garden. It never seemed to run low, and it still amazes me how much can pass through a chicken. We had a wagon for hauling this mess to the shed for mixing. In later years it was a treat for the grandchildren to ride in the wagon. Little did they know.........

... and now they do.

Everyone in the family knew Dad had a magical hand with gardening. His was always absolutely beautiful and bountiful, and many of the vegetables were larger than was typical for their kind. Obviously Dad's gift for gardening stayed with him throughout his life.

Through her daughter Connie, Aunt Mildred has shed some light on Dad's gardening skills. It seems that Dad, having grown up on a farm, took to having his own garden at the age of seven, apparently learning from his Dad, Oscar (Grandpa), and from his best friend, William, a black boy, the son of a man named Jefferson. Jefferson was the great grandson of a former slave of another family who came to the Daigles when all slaves were freed after the early 1800's. Slavery, as it was known in North Louisiana and in other Southern states was almost non-existent in South Louisiana from the early 1800s. Jefferson's wife Isabel helped with the farm by cooking the meals for the workers, and their daughter Souri helped in the house with the cleaning, cooking, and the children. Apparently William died as a teenager and was buried under a large oak tree on the front of the property. Grandpa and Dad had a headstone made and built a picket fence around the grave, and Dad planted sunflowers along the fence; the sunflowers having been one of William's particular talents.

Another story from Connie and Aunt Mildred is that Dad had provided the money necessary to complete the Daigle house in Lafayette when Grandpa had run out of money. Belle also remembers stories about Dad taking care of his family. Being the oldest child working, he felt it was his obligation to help provide, and the story goes back to an IOU he had signed with Grandpa when he was seven and just starting his garden. The IOU was for the land he used and the time spent working it instead of working on Grandpa's farm. Dad had kept the IOU for all those years. As a young man in his early twenties Dad returned the

IOU with the money to finish the house. Whether the IOU was just a joke grandpa played on Dad, who knows ... but maybe not. Aunt Anne told me that grandpa – her papa – was very strict, and although he rarely gave a whipping, his talks always brought the girls to tears. She also said that even though he was stern, he had another side, that of a very caring man.

Her stories to me about Dad were of a happy-go-lucky boy who sang and played jokes on people all the time. She was 99 when she told me these stories, so maybe she had Dad confused with someone else.

It should be noted that Dad was not one to trust a child to do much. For example, when we finally got our first gas powered grass mower in 1955, my job was to cut the field next to the house and the grass around it. Dad would walk behind me the entire way with Mom yelling at him to leave me alone and let me do it. She would tell him after we were finished, "If you're going to walk behind him the entire way, just do it yourself." I don't remember how long it was before Dad allowed me to cut the grass without him walking behind me. Oddly, he never followed me when I used the side blade or the manual mower.

We always had three full meals everyday, and always served at the exact same time everyday, and if you were late, the meal was gone. Mom and Dad usually spoke French to each other but not to us, and especially when they didn't want us to know what they were saying. Parents were discouraged from teaching their children French in those days.

If you spoke French, you were considered ignorant and backwoods.

Grandma Schexnayder spoke French, but she could speak English when she needed to. I remember her coffee, wrapped in cheese cloth and boiled for an hour or so before serving, and then only served in *demitasse* cups.

Her house is now part of the tourist stop at Sorrento, just south of I-10 on Highway 70.

Since Grandma Daigle lived in Lafayette and it was a long journey in our 48 Ford coupe to visit, I didn't spend much time with Grandma Daigle. There were no interstate highways, so you travelled on Highway 61 (Airline Highway) to Baton Rouge, then crossed the river and took Highway 190 to Opelousas, then down to Lafayette. Dad had a favorite place to stop and eat in Krotz Springs, and we always did.

As for other cousins my age, Lois Gail is who I remember. Daddy's sisters and brothers did visit us a lot, and a wonderful thing about his family was that no matter when or where they met, you always felt they were genuinely happy to see you.

This was my impression of Dad's sisters and brothers. Certainly Jules and Armand were genuine, and in the mid-1990s, when I assumed caretaking duties of the Daigle property in Lafayette, Aunts Anne, Mildred and Florence were some of the kindest people I have ever met. The nuns, Teresita (Hilda), Berchmans (Theresa), and Veronica (Leocadie) always made you feel they had a special bond with Dad and us, and you always knew they were holy people.

The car garage on the Garyville property was built into three sections, none of which housed a car. The outside sections housed the tools, garden implements, plows and farming equipment, and the innermost section was just a storage area for whatever needed storing, much like an attic.

Dad, Ruth, Helen, Nieces & Nephews

The middle section, the largest of the three, had shelves with a depth of two feet covering three sides and racks up the middle that started from just above the dirt floor up to the roof. It was on these shelves we ripened the tomatoes. They were picked just as they began to turn red, and then ripened inside the shed to protect them from the bugs, birds, and heat. Dad raised tomatoes in the late forties and early fifties, and since they were picked green before the birds and insects could ruin them, they were placed on these shelves to ripen, each section having tomatoes in different stages from green to ripe. Two days a week a large truck from New Orleans would arrive to load the tomatoes for sale in New Orleans. Dad would put arsenic in an old sock, tie it to a stick, then early in the morning as the dew was still on the plants, walk the rows shaking the sock, "powdering" the plants to kill the insects. It's a wonder he did not kill himself. Many people in Garyville raised vegetables which were sold in New Orleans; the Cascios and Monicas had large truck farms.

Original House In Garyville

We got our drinking and washing water from a large cypress cistern which stood just outside the back door of the house. In later years I would use some of that cypress to build a cradle for the new born babies entering the family. I think I was about 8 or 9 when Dad drilled a well and we got water piped into the house. Water pressure was an amazing thing. Francis, Lloyd, Carl, myself and Dad dug a trench from the well and across the pasture to Lloyd's house.

It was about this time that the backroom was added to the house; it had a toilet and wash basin and a couple of closets. Before the toilet, this was where the new washing machine had been installed, and Mom could take the clothes from its back door directly to the clothes lines. When later this became Dad's room to wash and get dressed, it relieved some of the pressure on the front bathroom, but by this time Ruth had gone off to college, so the pressure had eased up somewhat.

The house did not have air conditioning, which came many years later (in only one room) after everyone was grown and after much pleading with Dad. Mom never got to experience this marvel of modern technology. He finally broke down and got a window unit for the den, the room where everyone sat. We had a large attic fan, and at night the windows were cracked open and the moist, fog-laden air was pulled into the house. After Susan and I were married, I can remember Susan's first experience sleeping at the house with the attic fan turned on and the "wet" air came rushing in. It was almost as good as Dad putting the running lawn mower under the window to wake me to go cut the grass. It was a new experience for Susan.

Evolution, A Bedroom Added

Before Dad added the den, the steps led directly from the kitchen, and I can remember many mornings sitting on the steps eating small pieces of French bread broken into a bowl of chocolate milk.

Tea was never served without mint, and Mom grew it under the cistern. That's where she would hang the large cheese cloths of clabber to make cheese or cream cheese. About once every two months we would have to take our turn churning butter in the kitchen. I don't know for sure why no one wanted to do this, but everyone griped about it whenever it came their time to churn.

Pecans, do I remember pecans! We probably had twenty very large pecan trees on the property, and in season we spent every afternoon after school picking pecans, sacks and sacks of pecans. We sold about ninety percent of them. A truck would pass once a week and buy everything you wanted to sell, even the green and rotten ones. We found out later that the shells of those were used in gunpowder. We sold pecans at prices anywhere from 10 to 25 cents per pound.

Twice a week a truck would stop at everyone's house to sell fruit. Not only was fruit a treat, but the lagniappe was the real treat, guessing what would be given to you. Those days are long gone.

Vernon, Helen, Dad & Mom

It wasn't until I was eight that we got our first TV, so evenings before then we would all sit in the kitchen listening to the radio until about 8:00 or 8:30, then Mom would announce it was time to say the rosary. We prayed the rosary every night. Mom and Dad went to bed afterward, but we would listen to the radio a little longer or go outside and play for a little while.

I am not sure when television arrived in Garyville, but Carol J. Delery was the first that I knew to have one. He would put it in his store window at night, and many people would go to see the pictures, but no one could hear the sound through the glass.

Belle's recollection of television was that Torres got a TV before we did, and at night she and Carl would visit and watch TV there. The Bradys next door had moved to be with their children in New Orleans, so they rented their house to the Dusax family, and they had a television before we did. They had a daughter my age, so I was invited to watch the TV. A year or two later, after I turned eight, Mom and Dad finally got one. Mom would watch her "stories" and Dad had the news. Dad would come home at lunch, eat, watch a story, then nap for 30 minutes before going back to work. Most times the TV just stayed on with no one watching, with Dad sitting in his chair with a newspaper or magazine.

As kids we hunted and fished a lot, and me and a few other boys trapped in the winter for spending money. I still have a scar on my right index finger from my first experience taking a possum out of a trap. They do play possum. I got a Daisy Red Rider BB gun at age six, and then a 410 bolt action shotgun at seven. On the Christmas Day I received the shotgun, Mike (Vernon's son) and I were in the pasture on the side of the house, and Mike was insisting I let him shoot the gun, so I did. After his shot, we both took off running for the safety of the house after we heard the pellets hitting the Delery's roof. No one said anything and needless to say, Mike didn't ask to shoot again.

The deer hunting I did was not like Rene and Matthew hunt today, sitting in a tree waiting for a deer to come close and feed; that's like shooting cows. We hunted with shotguns in the swamp and had to chase the deer with dogs. It was a real effort to hunt deer, a real hunt, but everyone in town did it so it was just something you did. We also hunted rabbits, and my best friend Tim Hymel's family had two large packs of dogs, a pack of deer dogs and a pack of beagles to hunt rabbits. Many of the current day Schexnayders are rabbit hunters and still have rabbit dogs. In fact, Paul Melancon is rarely seen without a dog kennel in the back of his truck.

A few years after the new levee was built, many acres of land behind the new levee became a wonderful area to fish and hunt rabbits. The new ponds that were dug to build the new levee were fine for fishing, but nothing like the "old pond." Carl was the best sac-a-lait fisherman I have ever known. With just a cane pole and minnows, he could catch sac-a-lait (white perch) anywhere, anytime, but in the old pond, we all caught all we could carry.

Dad, Carl & Vernon

Vernon loved to fresh water fish, and in the fall he would spend many a day in Garyville fishing in the old pond. I can remember days when Dad, Carl, Vernon, and the kids would catch tubs of sac-a-lait and the kids would have to bring the tub home so the ladies could start cleaning while the men were still fishing. Those days are gone forever. The river itself was a great place to fish, and you never came home empty. Catfish (barbou) were most plentiful, but the occasional striped bass and gaspergou always added excitement.

The worse switching I ever got was because of fishing. Tim Hymel and I skipped school so we could move our boat from one pond to another to set lines. We were walking on top the levee with the boat over our heads when Mom spotted us, and that evening I got the willow switch.

Swimming in the river was always a fun time, and was a community activity. The idea was always to swim from one side to the other, and you had to think about it. The river's current in the summer months was always about 2 to 4 miles an hour (slow compared to the spring), so you had to plan your swim in order to end up on the far side, upriver from a turn. We really didn't swim across; we floated. If you didn't do it right you would get carried around the turn, which would add a long walk to your upriver walk so you could swim back across.

We would swim in the ponds, but for some reason not as often as in the river. I remember a family of Broussards who had several children with some learning handicaps, so to keep them safe in the river, a kind of pen was built for them, so there was no worry about them being carried away. They could have fun in the water just like the other kids. Besides the river itself, the land behind the levee was the equivalent of a very large playground. The woods, the ponds, and the river were enjoyed by all who lived in Garyville. It's hard to imagine such a peaceful and enjoyable place when looking at the area now.

When construction of the Kaiser Aluminum plant began, combined with the construction of Interstate 10 and its constant digging and hauling of sand, the area started losing its vitality and allure as a great playground. The river has long since claimed most of the land behind the new levee. But I used to spend hours alone, hunting, exploring, or just fishing the river or the ponds. Sitting and fishing was a very peaceful time.

Modern Day House

Marlin Perkins of the St. Louis Zoo had a TV show which was the precursor of the program *Animal Kingdom*. Perkins would come to Garyville many times a year to buy snakes, lizards, and black grasshoppers. It was very lucrative to sell the snakes, and along the Manchac road in springtime the black grasshoppers were everywhere. Perkins would pay 20 cents per foot for non-poisonous snakes and 40 cents per foot for poisonous snakes. Black grasshoppers were 4 cents each. It was very easy to catch snakes, especially water moccasins. An old wooden tomato crate with a missing side, placed at the edge of a pond or stream so minnows could collect under it, always yielded one or two moccasins. On one occasion I had a very large king snake that escaped in the house, got under the sofa, and wound itself in the springs underneath. With momma yelling at me about the snake, Carl and I had to take the sofa outside to get the snake from under it.

Across the river was the Blue Note, which hosted a gathering of musicians for jam sessions, and even with the levee between, on many Sundays you could hear the music as if it was next door. Many of the famous New Orleans musicians would be there every Sunday. Fats Domino was a regular, having been born somewhere close to the club.

Levee

Music was in our family. Vernon could play any instrument. Lloyd played several, including the piano by ear, and Carl could play it by ear as well; he could listen to a song, then sit down and within minutes be playing it. We were always amazed by that. Ruth was a great piano player and taught piano along with playing the organ at two churches on weekends. Belle and I got left out of the music business, although I did play the trumpet in the grammar school band and I played the piano a little, but singing was definitely out. My aptitude tests have always shown that I have artistic talent, but definitely not for music. In fact, I may be the only person ever asked to leave the Glee Club at St. Pauls.

Believe it or not, my Dad sang a great deal, but only when we were in the car. It was interesting to hear my aunts talk about Dad as a young man. They say he was a real joker, always playing pranks on people and just generally a happy-go-lucky guy.

My memories of Dad are of a much more serious man who spent long days working, either at home or in the schools. I cannot leave out the shaking. Because dad was 50 when I was born, my memories are of an older man. I realize now that I encounter this shaking (tremors); it can be embarrassing, and you never know if you should tell people why you are shaking or just let them think you had a very rough night.

By the time dad was in his mid sixties, the tremors were getting much more pronounced. It's actually a nerve disorder which bears the name *famille tremor,* and is predominant in men of French descent. Uncle Jules and Uncle Gabriel also had these tremors, and now myself as I approach old age. I have to laugh at myself sometimes when signing my name or handwriting something; I realize how similar my writing is to Dad's and that of Uncle Jules. Just a scribble of sorts. Letters to me from Uncle Jules are a real chore to read, and a manuscript he wrote in later life on the role abortion plays in the declining fabric of life is impossible to interpret. Looking at writing from Dad, Jules, and Gabriel Armand, it's amazing to see the handwriting of three different people in which you can't discern one from the other.

Dad was serious but he could also laugh. Mom did not come across as really serious, but she rarely laughed. Mom was incredibly hard working, taking care of the house and never complaining – that I knew of. I can remember being sick one day in the first grade, staying home from school and helping Mom with her new washing machine, the one with the wringers or rollers on top to wring the clothes dry. I got my hand caught, and by the time Mom arrived to turn it off, alerted by my screams, I was up to my shoulder. I got to hang clothes on the line rather than wring the water out of them.

I just don't remember Mom as the strict one, laying down the rules. My memories are of a more gentle person who spoke in softer tones when she wanted you to do something. However, she was quick to point out, "Wait until your Dad gets home."

Dad always told me, even as a very young boy, to make sure that I believed in something, because without a strong belief a person had no compass, moral, ethical, or otherwise, and no real sense of who he or she was. It was not until much later in life that I understood and appreciated the meaning of those words and those of my teachings in school: God, family, country, and state. I often wondered how I came to have such strong feelings for my country and the South. God and family were not in question. Anyone who prayed the rosary everyday, was required to attend every church service there ever was, and who was taught to respect their elders and women by default, had to respect God and family. The role of God in my life is critical to my well being.

Garyville was somewhat isolated from the other communities in the area. Lyons lay to the east of us and Mount Airy was to the west. When you went to Gramercy or Reserve you were really out of your territory. Thinking back on life in Garyville and being a country person, I can remember being in boarding school and as a freshman in high school and not knowing what a "gay" person was, and in those days I don't even know if the words gay or lesbian existed. My purpose is not to disparage gays and lesbians, only to show how different things were then.

My first encounter didn't happen until I was in high school, while driving down Peavine Road to go crawfishing. I noticed a car following me, and after I stopped a man followed me into the swamp. At first I had no clue, thinking only that this guy was looking for a place to crawfish, but I realized he didn't have any nets or any other apparatus needed for crawfishing. And then he began talking. I quickly notified him that if he did not want to become crawfish bait, he'd better move away from me fast, which he did. The pistol I carried probably had something to do with the speed of his retreat. I still wasn't sure what I had encountered. It's strange to equate my life in Garyville with how kids grow up today and what they learn from television. ED must be a way of life for most men today judging from the number of commercials aired on television.

Dad was principal of the school in Garyville before I was born. He later became an advisor to the school board, then a member for a short time, and then he became superintendent of Saint John the Baptist Parish. Mom taught occasionally at Saint Peter in Reserve.

One of Dad's duties was to visit adult education teachers in the schools, and I would go with him to these nightly meetings. I can remember hearing many kids and teachers alike saying upon our arrival, "Here comes the pipe man." Dad always had his pipe in his mouth. I'm not sure when he gave up smoking that pipe. He also smoked cigars during this time.

Each day when Dad came home from work he brought me a small treat such as a little piece of candy or a penny, so I would always be waiting for him and my treat. He would pretend to have forgotten it, then mysteriously produce it. This custom apparently was handed down from his Dad. In summers we all hung out at Boneno's service station. Dad would stop, and I could always coax ten cents out of him to get a Coke and a bag of peanuts. The peanuts were always dumped into the bottle and eaten as the Coke went down. I'm not sure why we did that, but everyone did it.

Gas was about 15 cents per gallon, and oil was filled in glass bottles from a large tank with a hand crank pump. Later, as a junior and senior in high school traveling to Covington to see Susan, I can remember filling up for about three or four dollars. Many days I would put in 25 cents' worth of gas to ride around town.

Carl had a real knack for killing rabbits with a car, a '51 Ford that he used as his own. He often came home with three or four rabbits he had run over in the cane fields. I guess it was sport for him.

He never took me on any of his four-wheel rabbit hunts, so I can assume that rabbits were not his primary objective in the cane fields.

Terry, Anne, Janice, Chuck, Neal & Dog

In growing up, two things about baseball and football come to mind. In baseball, even though we had barely enough to field a team, we always managed to win year after year. In one particular year, a sportswriter from New Orleans gave our coach, Ned Duhe, an offer: Garyville would play a best of five game series with the NORD champions from New Orleans; they had won the right to go to the Little League World Series. We knew nothing about New Orleans kids, but being scared probably helped us to win the series in just three games.

For football we had a little league team, but it was hard to find teams in the area to play us, so we ended up against many of the surrounding high school B teams. We did manage to win a game or two.

Garyville had a great sports tradition. Many of our boys went on to play for the Pelicans, a semi-pro team from New Orleans. In fact, after going off to St. Paul's, I was playing baseball in the men's league the summer between my freshman and sophomore years. While sliding into home plate, my cleats caught under the plate and I broke my ankle in three places. I remember Francis taking me to Lutcher, which had the closest hospital, and when I got on the x-ray table, I collapsed. The doctor said he couldn't do anything for me, so Francis brought me home to take a bath, then on to Baptist Hospital in New Orleans. My first trip to the big city. It was about 2:00 a.m. when we arrived, and my foot and leg were huge by this time. The doctor had to wait a day for the swelling to go down before he could operate to set my ankle back in place.

That doctor, Dr. Paul Accardo from LaPlace, went on to become one of the most prominent orthopedic surgeons in the South. I lucked out and got a good one.

Carl was a great athlete in his time, and I always wondered how far he could have gone had he been so inclined. In 1952, Reserve was playing Springhill for the state football championship, and Springhill had the great John David Crow, consensus All American at Texas A & M and then the pros. On one play Crow broke loose for a long run, and Carl ran him down from behind. Although Springhill won 6 - 0, the story grew to legend around Reserve and Garyville and followed Carl for years. The game became a battle between Carl and John David. The story circulated about how Carl ran down the great John David Crow, but this shouldn't have been a surprise, since Carl was the 100 and 200 yard state sprint champion at Reserve. If you ever wondered about the scars on Carl's face, they came from a neighborhood football game in Garyville. Carl ran into a barbed wire fence while attempting a tackle during the game. Dr. Johnson, a general practitioner, spent many hours stitching up his face. While in the Army Carl won the badminton doubles championship for the United States. After his discharge, myself and many others tried to get him to try out for football at Southeastern, but he would not.

Memories of food and cooking are not too vivid, except that Dad and Carl cooked all seafood and game while Mom cooked the chicken, pork, and beef. My recollection is that the food was good, but Grandma Daigle had everyone beat. She could cook anything, or at least that's how I remember it.

I don't recall my Grandma Schexnayder doing much cooking so I cannot comment on her cooking.

I never knew either of my grandfathers, both of them having passed on before I was born. My grandpa Schexnayder drowned in the river raising a shrimp box.

As a youngster, each summer I would spend two or three weeks at my Uncle Arthur's house. He was a cane farmer and farmed the Elina Plantation with four of my other uncles. Arthur had four children, MaryAnn, Arthur, Jeanie, and Lawrence. He lived on the river too, so things were not so different there except that he had many very large oak trees in front of his house. Those trees made great play areas. Back then Lawrence and I were the closest of the cousins, and in later years Arthur and I have developed a relationship for many years now.

I remember when Mary Lou and Linda were added to the mix at Grandma's house, but not so much playing with them as much as with the boys, especially Arthur's boys. In later years it was Uncle Edgar, Aunt Agnes's husband and the father of Mary Lou and Linda, who always advised Mom on issues involving the farm. Mom and her two sisters remained close even after they all moved away from Elina.

Back to food. Every Easter, Vernon (and sometimes Lloyd) would come to Garyville with his boys. On Good Friday morning we would all go crawfishing. We would come home before noon to boil the crawfish, and then everyone would go to church for the three o'clock Good Friday mass. On our return, everyone would peel crawfish and clean heads. On Saturday Mom would make the bisque while Dad made the stuffing for the heads. Everyone would then stuff the heads, and Mom would fry them in hog lard. In fact, there was always a white bowl of solidified hog lard on the stove to be used as needed.

Daigle / Giffin Nephews, Nieces and Cousins

Thinking back on my childhood growing up in Garyville, I had it pretty good. As for cooking, Vernon said in his book that it was Dad who cooked the game and Mom cooked everything else, which is pretty much how I remember it. I know both used basic seasoning, and both rubbed the meat with the seasoning hours before cooking it, so I can't really say if Mom or Dad influenced my love of cooking. When things are fresh from the garden, and real butter and hog lard is used, it is very difficult to make things taste bad.

Mom's fried chicken was great, and all she did was rub the chicken with a small amount of thyme and cayenne pepper, then she floured it with seasoned flour, salt, and black pepper. It's worth mentioning again that they used hog lard and real butter for everything. Next time you make biscuits, put bacon fat in the dough and see what happens to the biscuits. If you are really adventurous, add some cracklin crumbs.

Everything was cooked in hog lard except when Dad would fix my favorite meal. He would pick up fresh sausage when they made it at Verons, and just the smell made you hungry.

He poured one cup of water in a black iron fry pan, and then added the sausage with a few chopped onions, cooking it over a low fire. As the water would boil away, the grease from the sausage would be cooked out, and Dad would pour it over hot white rice. With hot French bread, this was my favorite meal.

The Backyard in Modern Times

A great story about community and food was the bakery in Garyville. All major bakeries in New Orleans bought their dough from this bakery. Dough was sold every Tuesday night, and everyone in town would line up to buy it. As a kid, this was a special treat. The dough was brought home and separated, with the bread dough wrapped in a canvas cloth and put aside. What remained was then rolled and cut into beignets, fried, put on a plate, and then melted butter and cane syrup was poured over them. What a treat! We did this many a Tuesday night.

The sugar mill at Garyville made syrup as well as sugar. This mill, the San Francisco Planting and Manufacturing Company, was owned by the Levet, Millet, and Rodrigue families, and their syrup to this day has never been equaled. But the real treat was the blackstrap molasses, which was the residue in the huge cooking kettles used for the syrup. The molasses couldn't be poured; it had to be scraped off the sides of the kettles. On hot French bread it was a real treat. The mill operated until Marathon purchased the land for an oil refinery.

After pouring off the syrup, sometimes the mill would let the kids go in and scrape the blackstrap off the insides of the kettles. The Rodrigues lived on the mill property and their son Winnie was my age, so we had a legitimate reason to be at the mill on a regular basis – plus Winnie's dad was one of the owners, which didn't hurt.

When Winnie and I went to St. Paul's as boarders in the ninth grade, I had barely been out of LaPlace. This was really foreign to me. All the boarders lived in one big dormitory, which housed about 120 boys on the third floor. The grades were issued at six week intervals, and everyone had to stand at the foot of their bed while one of the Brothers announced individual names. If your name was called, you had to go to the front of the dorm where a single bed was placed across the isle. Your failing grades were announced in front of God and everyone, and then you had the honor of pulling your pants down and laying across the bed while Brother gave you three whacks with a stout paddle for each failing grade. Poor Winnie; he had five Fs in the first six weeks. The next day he called his parents from the infirmary to ask them to come get him, and Winnie was history at St. Paul's.

During the ninth and tenth grades you got to go home three times during the school year: Thanksgiving, Christmas and Easter. Your parents could visit on every other Sunday. In the ninth grade, all the boarders and the Brothers would walk to downtown Covington on Friday nights to see a movie at the Star Theater. We did laundry after Saturday morning mass, then followed it with several hours of some sort of manual labor. At the time, the job was clearing trees and digging the now existing pond with shovels.

In those years the Brothers treated everyone as young men, and if you had a problem with one of them that couldn't be settled verbally, you had the option to go under the chapel, put on the boxing gloves, and take them on – if you dared. I must say there were a few who dared along the way. The boarders developed a special bond with the school, the brothers, and with each other. It still holds true today.

Some other memories were of the robin or blackbird (ricebirds) shoots from inside the house. Dad or Carl would spread cracked corn in an area on the levee and robins or blackbirds by the hundreds would gather in a pile. Through the open front window, one shot from the shotgun and literally a hundred birds, or so it seemed, were dead. Then came the scalding and never-ending plucking, but the gumbo was great. Bec croche would fly over in the late afternoons from the ponds or fields on their way to roost in the swamp, and Dad would stand against the barn and pick off three or four for gumbo.

Life in Garyville was easy, and people became life-long friends, as witnessed by the town reunions of recent years. A full town reunion was held about twenty years ago, and it was so successful that a few years later a "front" Garyville reunion was held also to great success.

At the front town reunion, people returned from all over the US, which was a real testament to the camaraderie that existed in the town. Everyone knew each other, and everyone were friends. Small country places were just like that.

I never knew my grandfathers. In looking back, I believe that I was fortunate that my dad was "old" when I was born, so I got a mixture of a father and grandfather. Fathers provide the discipline and grandfathers provide the wisdom of age. I often wonder what I would have learned if I been able to talk to Grandpa Daigle and Grandpa Schexnayder about their experiences growing up on a farm and living in rural Louisiana.

Near the end of Dad's life, I rode with him to the hospital in an ambulance, and as the medic was trying to get him to lie down, he said, "I'm going to sit up so I can get my last look at my town." Typical of Dad.

In his early 80s, while coming out of Poleto's grocery, a step collapsed and Dad broke his leg. He would not allow a cast to be put on it. He wrapped it himself and proceeded to make a crutch from a broom stick, with a piece of 2" x 10" board he carved to fit his arm. When he had surgery for an ulcer and 50% of his stomach was removed, he raised holy hell in the hospital because they would not allow him to walk to the operating room. I can also remember, when cleaning wasp nests from the pecan trees and being stung repeatedly, how amazed I would be that the stings didn't seem to have any effect on him. He appeared oblivious to the pain.

When Lloyd was dying, he had a wish to return to Garyville. His reason was that it was such a peaceful place, and one of good memories. He told me he thought of Garyville often, and it always made him feel better. When Ruth was dying, she asked me to tell her about my life in Garyville, about growing up in a peaceful and happy time. That request by Ruth is what started this recording of my memories of growing up in Garyville. Maybe when people are at the end of their lives they always want to return to the place of their early learning, but I do believe Garyville was an easy, happy place filled with contentment. I have no bad memories; only happy, carefree ones. Maybe it was not Garyville, but our home.

WHAT IS A FAMILY
It's a Father's strength and wisdom
And a Mother's tender love
And the innocence of childhood
Held with God's strength from above

It's the source of joy and laughter
Jokes and secrets, smiles and tears
It's a wealth of treasured memories
That grow dearer with the years

It's a warm and special feeling
Binding hearts to hearts forever
In a spirit of belonging
Neither time nor miles can take away!

As an adult I have been privileged to visit many countries; Azerbaijan, Georgia, Armenia, Kazakhstan, Turkmenistan, Uzbekistan, Tajikistan, Russia, India, Ukraine, UAE, Great Britain, France, Germany, Belgium, Luxembourg, Italy, Switzerland, Canada, Mexico, Paraguay, Brazil, Venezuela, Puerto Rico and Cyprus.

Associated Documents

There are two manuscripts, one a letter written by Quorum Daigle, which mistakenly crosses two families and is therefore in error in some parts, but correct in others. Etienne was the first to come to Louisiana in 1717 or 1720. Two brothers, Chevalier and Alexander Daigle, arrived with the Acadian exiles approximately 40-50 years later after Etienne had moved from St. Charles Parish to Plaquemine Brulee. They could have been related to Etienne if they were descendants of Olivier, and then only if Olivier had been related to Jean "L'Allemand" D'Aigle.

There is a much larger unpublished manuscript of the Daigle family titled *Etienne Daigle*, written by Norwood Marcy Lyons. This manuscript was carefully studied by Uncle Jules, and he pronounced it to be the most correct of the stories regarding the Daigle family. This manuscript also matches the genealogy of the Daigle Family Association and the Quebec Daigle family records. Her manuscript states that Etienne arrived in New Orleans in 1717, and a marriage license shows Etienne marrying Suzanne d'Esperon in 1721. This seems to tie the arrival of Etienne between 1717 and 1720 to other records of the time, including church records in St. Charles Parish, which also tie Etienne Daigle to a relationship with the Schexnayders in the area weat of Taft and Vacherie areas before Etienne moved the family to Plaquemine Brulée (Church Point). The error of this manuscript, as pointed out by Uncle Jules, was the tying of the Olivier Daigle family to the Jean Daigle family. The Olivier Daigles came to Louisiana during the Grand Derangement, and our family arrived many years earlier. As stated earlier, the Quebecois French Daigles (Jean Daigle's family) arrived in Louisiana some 50 years or so before the Olivier Daigle family, which was expelled from Canada back to France during the Grand Derangement.

Other Daigles, such as the brothers Chevalier and Alexander, who had remained in Canada when Etienne came to Louisiana, followed some years later, and records indicate they went straight to Plaquemine Brulée when arriving in Louisiana. That suggest a relationship between these Daigles and Etienne, but that direct tie is unknown.

The history of the Daigles and Schexnayders as well as the sugar cane farming history of the Schexnayders up to the present day, are both truly a part of the overall history of the state. As of June 25, 2011, Arthur and Gary Schexnayder's farm operations are now run by cousins who farm in spots from Vacherie to Donaldsonville. In Pointe Coupee Parish, Raymond Schexnayder & Sons is one of the area's largest farmers, farming mostly soybeans. The Schexnayders have been farming sugar cane since it started in Louisiana in the late 1700s, almost 300 years. Prior to the farming of sugar cane, indigo and vegetables were the primary crops. The Daigles and the Schexnayders are true pioneers of Louisiana, our nation, and the family history is a True Louisiana Legacy.

DATA SOURCES & REFERENCES

Vacherie, History and Genealogy, Elton J. Oubre

Precious Gems from Faded Memories, Pictorial History of St. John the Baptist Parish, Gerald Keller, Lisa Keller, Darroch Watson

History of St. John the Baptist Parish, Rt. Rev. Msgr. Jean Eyraud, Donald Millet

Schexnayder The Family, Mike Schexhayder

Etienne Daigle, Unpublished Manuscript, Norwood Marcy Lyons

St. Louis Cathedral Archives, New Orleans, Book of Marriages 1720 - 1730

St. Charles Borromeo Catholic Church, Destrehan, LA, Marriages and Baptisms and Death

Southwest Louisiana Records 1756 - 1810, Rev. Donald J. Hebert

Census Tables of Louisiana 1699 - 1732, Charles R. Maduell, Jr.

General Census of All Inhabitants of New Orleans and Environs, 1721, Le Sieur Diron *Louisiana Census & Militia Lists 1770 - 1789,* Albert Robicaux

The German Coast, Civil Records of St. Charles Parish & St. John the Baptist Parish, 1804 - 1812, Glenn R. Conrad

The Catholic Church in Louisiana, Roger Baudier

Our Lady of the Sacred Heart Catholic Church, Church Point, Louisiana.

Rev. Msgr. Jules Daigle, *South Louisiana Cajuns,* unpublished manuscript

The Advocate, *Mulatto Bend Settlement,* 2013

Zerangue, Zeringue, Zyrangue and Allied Families, Agnes Rita Zeringue Foreman 1979

Mississippi Valley Melange, History & Genealogy of the Territory of Orleans, Winston De Ville 1995

World Book of Daigles, Halbert's Family Heritage

Down Among the Sugar Cane, The Story of Louisiana Sugar Plantations and Their Railroads, W. E. Butler 1980

The World's Last Mysteries, Readers Digest

Cajun French Self Taught, Rev. Msgr. Jules Daigle, Seven Dolores Church

Cajun French I, French in Vermillion and Surrounding Parishes, James Donald Faulk

Vieux Vacherie, the Madstone of Vacherie, Mrs. Eddie Oubre

Louisiana Under 10 Flags, Louisiana Secretary of State

Facts About Louisiana, Louisiana Secretary of State

Acadian Journal, T. Hebert 1997

Societe Francaise d'Heraldique et de Sigillographie, 113 Rue de Courcelles, Paris 17, France

Association de la Famille Daigle

Societes de Genealogie Canadienne, Francaise

Holy Family Parish, Daigle, Maine 1906 - 2000 94 Years of Ministry, Laurel J. Daigle

Castellanos, *New Orleans As It Was*

No Cross, No Crown; Black Nuns in Nineteenth Century New Orleans, Sister Mary Bernard Diggs Louisiana State Library Press, 1981

The Churches and the Negro in New Orleans 1850 - 1860 Liliane Crete

Daily Life in Louisiana 1815 - 1830 Patrick Gregory Tannenbaum,

Slave and Citizens: The Negro in the Americas, Alfred Knopf, 1947

Black Code, American Catholics and Slavery, 1789 - 1866

Jean Pierre Daigle, Ste-Therese, Quebec, Canada

The Daigle Legacy, Lynette LeBlanc Kleinpeter

Lafayette Parish Historical Records, St. John Catholic Parish

Msgr. Jules Daigle, Opelousas Daily World, New Iberia Press, January 16, 1998

The Eagles Wings, Volume 2, Number 2, The Daigle Family News Letter

Les Archives Pere Clarence d'Entremont, Voyage to Nova Scotia 1731 Weinstein & Gagliano, *The Shifting Deltaic Coast*

The Indian Tribes of North America, Swanson

A Comparative View of French Louisiana, Brasseau

Carte Particulaire Du Cours Du Fleuve Mississipy, Broutin

Civil Records of St. Charles and St. John the Baptist Parishes, St. Charles Borromeo Church

State of Louisiana History, St. Charles, St. John the Baptist and St. James Parishes

History of St. John the Baptist Parish, Hope Haven Press 1939

Jay Schexnaydre, President of the Genealogical Research Society of New Orleans, Webmaster of the German-Acadian Coast Historical & Genealogical Society

Edward Oscar Daigle, Jr.

Edward Oscar Daigle Jr. was born in Garyville, Louisiana on September 27, 1944 to Leah Schexnayder and Edward Oscar Daigle. He married Susan A. Ayers of Covington, Louisiana on August 3, 1963. Together they have four Children - two sons and two daughters with currently ten (10) grandchildren.

Edward began his career working in the marine oil and gas industry and traveled worldwide as a welding and coatings inspector, and construction superintendent. In 1979, he became the chief executive for a company which employed in excess of 500 people.

Over the years, Mr. Daigle has served as the chief executive for several companies, and from 1989 through 1998 he traveled extensively in Russia to begin development of a technology exchange company with the Russian Space Agency.

Edward is the author of several patents and patent applications and has published papers on the subject of plasma metals processing, using hydrogen plasma.

Honors received include:
- Governor's Council for a Better Louisiana
- Who's Who, Business & Industry Southwest USA
- Board Director, Iberia Parish Chamber of Commerce,
- Honorary Secretary of State, 1986
- President of Louisiana Import/Export Assoc.
- 2004 Horace Pops Award, WAI for Technical Literature

Printed in the USA
CPSIA information can be obtained
at www.ICGtesting.com
LVHW050541260624
783966LV00013B/980